BANK OF DAVE

How I Took on the Banks

DAVE FISHWICK

2 4 6 8 10 9 7 5 3

First published in 2012 by Virgin Books, an imprint of Ebury Publishing

A Random House Group Company

www.randomhouse.co.uk

Addresses for companies within The Random House Group Limited can be found at www.randomhouse.co.uk/offices.htm

The Random House Group Limited Reg. No. 954009

A CIP catalogue record for this book is available from the British Library

The Random House Group Limited supports The Forest Stewardship Council (FSC®), the leading international forest certification organisation. Our books carrying the FSC label are printed on FSC® certified paper. FSC is the only forest certification scheme endorsed by the leading environmental organisations, including Greenpeace. Our paper procurement policy can be found at www.randomhouse.co.uk/environment

Text design and typesetting by carrdesignstudio.com
Printed and bound in Great Britain by CPI Group (UK) Ltd, Croydon, CR0 4YY

ISBN: 9780753540787

To buy books by your favourite authors and register for offers, visit www.randomhouse.co.uk

CONTENTS

'It is well enough that people of the nation do not understand our banking and money system, for if they did, I believe there would be a revolution before tomorrow morning.'

Henry Ford, founder of the Ford Motor Company

'Rule number 1: Never lose money.
Rule number 2: Never forget Rule number 1.
Rule number 3: Never give up.
Rule number 4: Never, *ever* give up.'

Dave Fishwick, founder of
David Fishwick Van and Minibus Sales

I would like to dedicate this book
to my dear wife and best friend, Nicky

INTRODUCTION

The story of the Bank of Dave is not just a story about a bank, or about a bloke called Dave. First and foremost, it's a story about people. It's a story about you.

All businesses are about people. They're about the people who have the ideas and the people who run them, the people who work for them and the people who buy from them. A business isn't just a balance sheet or a stock price. It's not just a commodity to be bought and sold and speculated upon. Think of your local pub. What makes it what it is? Is it the profit and loss account, or the owner's dividends? Or is it the lads and lasses who serve behind the bar; the chef who cooks your scampi and fries; the lorry driver who delivers the beer; the brewer who brews it in the first place; you, having a couple of pints on a Friday night?

Without people, there are no businesses. End of story.

All banks are about people, too. Not just the high-flying city types with their pinstripe suits and their bulging wallets, but ordinary folk. Teachers and doctors. Dustmen and checkout attendants. Gardeners, hairdressers, tea ladies and social workers. Without these people, and the money they keep in their bank accounts, however little, there would be no banks. There are plenty of city types out there who will try to tell you that their enormous bonuses and champagne lifestyles are somehow down to their own brilliance and hard work. They're not. They're down to you, and to the money you put in their hands. Somewhere along the line, a lot of people have forgotten that. I think it's time they started to remember it, and I don't believe I'm the only one who thinks this way.

My name's David Fishwick, and I'd like to think I'm as ordinary as the next fella. Don't get me wrong: I've done OK. But I wasn't born with a silver spoon in my mouth. I didn't have a fancy education that could teach me how to bamboozle people with complicated words and figures and make them think I was better than them. I was born and bred in Nelson, Lancashire, which is about as far as you can get from Oxbridge or the Square Mile – and I'm not just talking about distance. Back then it was the most depressed suburb of one of the poorest towns in the country. Things haven't changed much. The house I grew up in has been condemned and knocked down. There was a time when, quite literally, I didn't have the price of a chip butty in my back pocket. Things are different now. I know I'll never have to worry about money again. I live in a large house in a hundred acres of countryside, and my Ferrari is parked next to my own helicopter, which I fly whenever I get the chance. But you're as likely to find me drinking a mug of tea in a cafe on Burnley High Street as you are to find me eating my dinner in some swanky restaurant. At heart, I'd like to think I'm still that kid from Nelson.

So what would that kid from Nelson have thought about the way banks have behaved over the past few years? What would he have said if you'd asked him? He wasn't educated, and he didn't have much experience of the real world. But he did have a healthy dose of common sense. I'm sure he'd have realised that there was something not quite right about buying and selling things with money that didn't really exist. He'd have raised an eyebrow if you'd told him that someone might be paid millions of pounds for doing deals that lost an unimaginable fortune made up of other people's savings. He'd have been entirely perplexed by the idea that the ordinary members of the public from his impoverished, run-down community should end up paying for these people's mistakes. And I'm sure he would have found it almost impossible to understand how anyone – *anyone* – could lose themselves £50 billion. He'd be scratching his head just like everybody else. He's still scratching his head now.

I understand a lot more about business now than I did then, but I still find it hard to comprehend what has happened and how the banks have got themselves – and us – into such a terrible mess. And I can't help thinking the banks *like* it that way. The more complicated their world seems to you and me, the more we tell ourselves that we could never understand it, the freer they are to be reckless with our money, and to pretend that their cock-ups aren't cock-ups at all, but the inevitable consequences of a world we know nothing about.

The trouble is, that's bollocks.

When I decided to set up the Bank of Dave, my plan was

simple. I wanted to show that there was a better way to do banking. I wanted to show that the suspicion we all share that they have had it too good for too long is right. To do this, I would aim to pay ordinary people many times more interest than they can get anywhere else. I would guarantee every pound they put in with a pound of my own money, so that the risk was mine, not theirs. I would lend money to local businesses who, through no fault of their own, couldn't get credit anywhere else. And to show that banking doesn't have to be rocket science, I would try to get my bank into profit in 180 days. Anything I made at the end of that period would go to charity.

At the end of the day, I hoped to show that the worlds of business and banking and commerce aren't complicated. They're simple. If a lad from Nelson who grew up without a pot to piss in can get his head around them, anyone can. What *isn't* simple is getting the Establishment to admit this. I knew, when I first thought about setting up my own bank, that it would be an uphill struggle. But I could never have imagined just how hard it would be, or just how many obstacles would be thrown in my way. After all, it would be an embarrassment if an ordinary person managed to take on all those big established banks at their own game and win, wouldn't it?

But what they have failed to realise is that their profits and their bonuses and their lavish lifestyles are all built on the hard work of others. And that's something I *do* know about. My hope is that by the end of this book you'll have learned a thing or two about business that you can put into practice; and that you'll have learned a thing or two about how the banks work, what they've done with your money, and how it's possible to take a stand against them. The story of how *I* took on the banks starts with the story of my own journey through the world of business, and I could never have set up the Bank of Dave if I hadn't taken away a few pieces of know-how from the dog-eat-dog world of buying and selling...

PART 1

THE WORLD ACCORDING TO DAVE

This isn't one of those books that's written just so that the author can bang on about himself long past the point where everyone's bored to tears and wishing he'd just put a sock in it.

I won't be telling you what my favourite breakfast cereal is, or the name of the first girl I snogged. I'll leave all that to the shiny celebs in *Hello!* magazine.

But I *am* going to tell you a few things about my life in business. About the way I see the world, and how I go about things. The world according to Dave might be different to the world according to lots of other people, and my way's not the only way. I suppose every businessman has their own set of rules, many of them learned at fancy business schools that give you lots of letters after your name so that you can show everybody how clever you are. Maybe these places really do teach you what you need to run a successful business. I wouldn't know, because everything I've learned has been at the coalface.

What I do know is this: the world according to Dave is a straightforward place. A place where there isn't much room for bullshit. When I started down the path of setting up the Bank of Dave, I soon learned that the world of banking is as far from being bullshit-free as it's possible to get. In order to cut through the crap, I would have to draw on everything I'd learned during twenty years in business. I also lost count of the number of people who told me it couldn't be done because I didn't have the right qualifications, the right experience, the right this, the right that... Well, I'm not knocking qualifications and I'm not knocking experience. But I do think people are quick to forget the benefits of a bucketful of common sense, and I'm sure there are plenty who'd do well to remember that the best way to learn about business is by running one. I've been doing that since I was sixteen, and I've picked up a thing or two on the way.

Don't Let the Bastards Get You Down

I did terribly at school. Worse than terribly. If you were to ask my teachers what little David Fishwick was like, they would tell you I was a loser. A bum. Useless. Academically speaking, I was without question one of the worst pupils in the school. Why was that? Hard to say – perhaps some people just aren't cut out for formal education, though it didn't help that I was bullied something rotten for the first twelve years of my life.

I was a tiny kid, shorter than everyone. I wasn't very clever. I wasn't very good at sport. I wasn't very good at music. I wasn't very good at *anything*. In games lessons, when the other kids picked out their teams, I was always the last to be chosen – I was forever hearing the phrase, 'Do we have to *have* him, he's *shit!*' Or I was used as a bargaining tool, 'We'll only take Fishwick if we can have him over there who's *good* at football...'

You don't have to hear people telling you that you're rubbish very many times before you start to believe it. And yet it wasn't just the words that hurt me; it was the sticks and stones too. Being so small, I was an easy and obvious target for some of the bigger kids. Pretty soon, I grew accustomed to being used as a punchbag. I grew accustomed to the bruises and the humiliation. To absorbing one blow after another, day after day after day.

Little wonder, then, that I decided pretty early on that school wasn't the place for me. It wasn't a place where I went to learn; it was a place where I went to be hit and teased. At least, that's what it was for the first twelve years of my life. After that, things became different.

A few years ago, I was invited back to the school when they were closing it down. My profile in the local community had risen, and I was well known as a businessman who was getting on all right. It seemed appropriate to them that I should be the last person to walk out of the school, to close the door on its eighty-year history before the bulldozers moved in and a brand spanking new school was built in its place. I walked around that building filled with nostalgia, remembering every last cupboard and doorway and blackboard as if I'd left only yesterday. The last thing I did before walking out of that condemned building was ask for my photograph to be taken by a particular window in a particular corridor on the ground floor. Like the rest of the school, this location wasn't much to look at. Bland. Institutional. You could see why they were going to knock it down. But to me, that spot had great meaning because it was here, when I was twelve years old, that my life changed.

There was one lad – I won't give his name – six months younger than me but a hell of a sight bigger. In his own little world he was the tough guy, and it was his habit to prove that by laying in to me whenever he had the opportunity. For a long time, I assumed what everyone else assumed: he *was* a tough guy, and it would be suicide to stand up to him, even if I had the guts to do it.

But on the day in question, all that changed.

I was walking along this corridor, with a satchel slung over my shoulder, when this lad decided to have another crack at me. He leered in my direction and lumbered over, his fist already clenched. He punched me on the side of the face. It was hard, even by his standards. It hurt.

I remember the next few seconds as if they were yesterday. As I replay them in my mind, they seem to happen in slow motion. I dropped my satchel and, as it fell to the floor, I clenched my fist. And then, with all the strength I could put behind it, I hit him back.

And I hit him.

And I hit him.

I hit him until I couldn't hit him any more.

This lad did try to retaliate in between, but because I'd been bullied for so many years and hit so many times, I realised it didn't hurt any more, or at the very least, I didn't care if it did. I wasn't made of glass. I wouldn't shatter. So I might take a few bruises away from the encounter: So what? This lad could come at me all he liked. I wasn't going to stand for being bullied any more.

It was a turning point in my life. I realised I *could* fight back. Not just people my own size, but the big guys too. And more to the point, I could win.

I've had lots of fights since that day, some with my fists, some legal. I've had real mountains to climb, but I've never again allowed myself to be bullied. If anybody comes anywhere near me, I'll set about them in an instant. And it's a lesson I've carried with me: bullies aren't used to people fighting back. They've probably never been hit before, or had their bluff called in the cold light of day, because they're used to being the ones who do the hitting. Of course, bullies aren't always just individuals. Sometimes they hunt in packs; sometimes they are seemingly respectable businessmen; sometimes they are faceless corporations; sometimes they are huge financial institutions. But it doesn't matter if they are spotty, aggressive kids or major international banks. Like somebody once said: the bigger they are, the harder they fall. I've had to remember that countless times over the years, but never more so than when I started taking on the banks at their own game. Of all the bullies I've come across – and there have been a few – the banks are perhaps the biggest.

But I also know this: like all bullies, they don't like it when you hit back.

Put Your Back Into It

Finding my fists may have done wonders for my twelve-year-old confidence, but it didn't do much for my schoolwork. I don't believe I was especially stupid, but I was perhaps slightly slower to catch on to certain things than the others. Once you get a little bit behind, it's easy to get further behind. I'd have benefited from some one-to-one tuition. Nowadays this is something I can – and do – afford, but back then I was just one little face in a tough state school in Nelson, Lancashire. There was as much chance of me having one-to-one tuition as there was of the headmaster walking starkers across the school yard.

The teachers thought I was thick. Everyone thought I was thick. I just thought I was different and as a result found that I couldn't be bothered with anything to do with school. So I was forever skiving off. The teachers just thought I was a waster, that the only thing likely to happen to me would be that I'd just get into trouble. They soon forgot about me, and I fell off the radar while they concentrated on the clever kids.

I left school with a big old chip on my shoulder, thinking it had all been a waste of time. I was sixteen years old with nothing but three CSEs to my name and a pile of reports telling me how useless I was at maths and sport and everything else they taught at school. But I look back now and I wonder if I really was so stupid; maybe I was just good at different things. I definitely seemed to have a bigger dose of common sense than most of my contemporaries, and I certainly wasn't afraid of hard work. A friend of mine had a window-cleaning round, and I used to help him out. I also had four paper rounds: one in the morning, one at teatime, one on Sunday and one delivering the free newspaper.

I was, slowly but surely, learning a work ethic, which was bolstered by my dad. He had a work ethic in spades. I barely saw him during the week when I was growing up, because he always had two jobs. He'd get up at half past four in the morning and walk to his first job which was on a local farm. He'd work there, milking the cows and doing whatever else it is that farmers do, until half past one. He'd then walk to a local mill, where he'd work from two till ten. I was asleep when he left the house; I was asleep when he got back. And I can't remember a time when I didn't have the work ethic that he drilled into me, perhaps without even knowing he was doing it. He taught me that nothing gets achieved if you don't put your back into it. That work ethic is a precious thing. It was just a matter of deciding how it was to be utilised.

Find What You Want to Do, and Do It

Dad was adamant that I should be a builder. It was a well-meant ambition. My brother was a really wonderful joiner, and Dad's grand plan was that if I learned the building trade, the two of us could build houses together. That way, we'd never be short of work. It was a good idea, with one small flaw: I could barely nail two bits of wood together. That didn't faze Dad. It was a Thursday when I left school at sixteen with my rubbish CSEs, quite looking forward to a few months off while I came to my own decisions about what to do with my life; come Monday morning, I was sitting on a builder's truck, freezing my bollocks off despite the old black donkey jacket wrapped around me, flask stuck in one pocket, sandwiches in another. There was a hierarchy on that grimy pick-up: the old-timers got to sit up front in the warmth of the cab; the new kids sat on the back in the open air, with the sand and muck in our faces and the wind blowing through us. I remember thinking on that Monday morning that maybe school wasn't so bad after all.

I was apprenticed to a builder called Frank Byrne as part of the Youth Training Scheme which operated then. One day a week I'd go to college to learn bricklaying. The rest of my time was spent on building sites. My first building job was in a local cotton wool factory where some of the expensive machinery had to be locked away at night in a secure location; we were here to build the lock-up. The factory stank. As I walked in, I saw one of the workers stuffing bags full of cotton wool and placing them on a conveyor belt. That was the only thing he did all day long. It looked mind-numbing, and made me wonder what the hell I was doing there.

I was a useless builder, just like I'd been a useless student. I hated the work, and I didn't see eye to eye with my boss. He used to wear a flat cap with flaps that covered his ears, and he was forever ripping it off, throwing it to the ground, stamping and yelling and screaming at me for getting things wrong. And there's no doubt that I *did* get things wrong. I couldn't lay bricks, I couldn't mix cement, I couldn't plaster; but I *was* a good little worker, so most of my days were spent labouring, a bucket of cement in each hand, going up ladders all day long, unloading wheelbarrows full of bricks into skips as I tried to keep up with the big guys. Proper, hard graft. But all the time I was there, my mind was somewhere else. Perhaps that was why I didn't pick things up as quickly as I could have; perhaps I was just never cut out to be a builder. Whatever the truth, I knew that this wasn't for me. It didn't take me long, however, to find out what was.

I had a little 50cc motorbike. I'd bought it myself, out of my own wages – I think I paid around thirty-five quid for it – and I remember riding it up to Burnley car auctions. I don't remember what drew me there. I just remember sitting on a table where somebody had left half a cup of tea, drinking what was left of the brew and watching the cars going through. I was transfixed. I knew, without even knowing why, that I wanted to be something to do with it. For me, cars were the future.

Some of the lads I met at college got me into boxing, and a good deal of my free time was spent at the local boxing gym, a dirty, sweaty place where I met some real characters and started to get a bit fitter. That side of my life was fine, but the building sites I hated. I *hated* going to work; I *knew* it wasn't the career for me. There's a rebellious side to my nature that I still have today; back then, though, it was deep in me. I loathed being told what to do, but I simply didn't have enough money to get me out of it. I knew I wanted to get into buying and selling cars, but without any funds to do it, it was just a pipe dream.

And funds were scarce. More than scarce. I had no money to buy anything with. I took home around twenty-seven quid a week on the YTS from working on the building sites, plus a few quid from Frank, and I gave my mum twenty quid of that for my board and lodging. The rest went on running my little motorbike. One day I walked into a chip shop in Nelson and asked the woman behind the counter for a chip butty. It was the only thing I was going to get to eat that day, and as she was making it I realised I was a couple of pence short. I explained the problem to her, and asked if she would just take a couple of chips out of the roll, fully expecting her to tell me not to worry about it and to waive the couple of pence I couldn't pay her. She didn't. She removed a few chips from the butty before handing it to me. It was such a mean-spirited thing to do that as I walked out of that chip shop, I silently vowed that one day I would have enough money to go back and buy it.

I knew what I wanted to do. I also knew something that, for many people, takes a long time to learn. Just talking about doing something is no good. You've got to put your words into action. Plans and dreams are nothing more than that if you don't *do* anything about achieving them. Like someone once said, you've got to be in it to win it.

And so, for the first time in my life, I started to think outside the box.

If You Don't Believe In Yourself, Nobody Else Will

If I was going to buy and sell cars – and I knew this was something I could make a success of – I needed to get my foot on the ladder. So I went around all the garages in Nelson that sold vehicles and took part exchange. Punters would bring in an old car, and drive away in something a little newer. The value of the part-exchange vehicles was about sixty or seventy pounds. It doesn't sound a lot now, but bear in mind that my week's wages were around £27. I made the garages an offer: let me take one of these crummy old part-exchange cars away, do it up and sell it on. I can't afford to pay you, I explained, but as soon as I've made the sale, I'll bring you your £70. I was only sixteen years old, and I can't have come across as a very safe bet to the car dealerships I approached. But in the end, I pitched my idea to one bloke in a back-street garage in Nelson. 'All right,' he said. 'I'll let you do that.' He trusted me, and I was determined to take my chance.

I took a car away with me and worked hard cleaning it up. I silver-sprayed the wheels, I blackened up the tyres, I scrubbed it and painted it – and all this I did at night while I was working on building sites during the day. When the car was gleaming, I advertised it in the local paper, and sold it for £97. The minute I had the money in my hand, I jumped on my motorbike, rode over to the house of the man who'd lent me the car and hammered on his door. The moment he opened up, I handed over the £70. I think he was astonished to see me – I was just a punt for him, and he didn't *really* expect me to be able to sell the car. But I'd never had any doubt, and I always intended to pay him back immediately.

I'll always be grateful to that man. But I also knew that if he *hadn't* given me the chance, I'd have found someone else who would – I believed in myself, and it was one of the earliest and most vital lessons I learned: if you don't believe in yourself, nobody else will. Other people will jump in the water if you jump in first. But crucially, it took somebody to give me a bit of leg-up to realise, finally, that there was something I could do well. Nearly twenty-five years later I'd find myself on the other side of the fence, seeing individuals with potential and talent ready to spread their wings if only someone would give them the helping hand they needed. I'd also see that the institutions who *should* be doing that – the banks – were not.

Money Talks

In that one trade, I'd made as much money as I earned in a week on the building sites. For Frank, I was truly grafting, carrying buckets of cement up and down ladders all day. The idea that I could make just as much money from tinkering with a car in the street outside our house for a few hours of an evening was an eye-opener.

I asked the garage man if I could take another car. 'Of course you can!' So I did it again. Before long I was selling one car a week, then six cars a month. All of a sudden, I had three hundred quid in my pocket. So now, instead of asking if I could take a car on spec and pay for it if and when it sells, I could start to negotiate: if I paid for the car first, and took the risk on whether it sold and what for, could I have it for less? I certainly could. I had very quickly learned, and at an early age, one of the most important lessons in business: money talks (and bullshit walks!). You get a much better deal if you can pay for something up front.

The cash I had to spend gradually increased. Soon I was able to go to the car auctions, not as a bystander cadging half-drunk cups of tea, but as a punter with money in my pocket. What I didn't have, though, was a driving licence – don't forget that I was only sixteen – so I had to take my brother along to move the vehicles I bought and sold around for me. If he couldn't come, I'd try to move the cars myself. I'll never forget trying to do a handbrake start in an old Capri that had been parked on a hill. I just couldn't do it, and the vehicle started rolling down the hill with me inside it, worrying that I was going to get banned before I'd even got going.

The Bit In The Middle

I didn't get banned, and the minute I was seventeen I took my test, which made life a whole lot easier. I was still working on the building sites, but I was also working for myself – and earning a lot more from my own endeavours than from the day job. Buying and selling, I realised, was the way forward, because it removed the element of labour. There were only so many hours in the day I could carry buckets of cement up ladders, but there was no limit to the number of cars I could buy and sell. If I could buy a car cheaper than someone else was willing to pay for it, the bit in the middle was profit for me. Buy cheap, sell dear. Buy cheaper and the middle bit increases; sell dearer and the middle bit increases. There was no way I was able to get a bank loan in those days, even when I was old enough. I had no credit history or banking history. I used to max out on three or four credit cards, raising maybe £1,500 to buy and sell a car, before paying back the credit card. The bit in the middle was mine.

Plenty of people will try to tell you that this concept of the bit in the middle is rocket science. It isn't, but it is the secret of any business, not just cars. I learned it early. As my business career progressed, I saw people trying to complicate matters. But there's nothing complicated about retail. I soon learned to ignore the bank managers who kept telling me that I needed to increase my turnover, that this was the great secret of a healthy business. Rubbish. Turnover is for vanity; profit is for sanity. You can't spend turnover when you go down to Asda for your big shop. You can only spend profit. In business, the only thing that matters is the bit in the middle. If Company A has a turnover of £100 million and a profit of £500 (this is more common than you'd think), and Company B has a turnover of £1,000 and a profit of £501, who's done better?

I don't think you need to be Richard Branson to answer that question…

So why were those bank managers always telling me to increase my turnover? Why did the idea of turnover make them happier than the idea of profit? Simple. More turnover means more money in the bank for them to do with as they wish. That's good business sense for the bankers, but it's not good business sense for you. And if that sounds like the banks – who should be supporting us because it's thanks to us that they exist in the first place – aren't looking out for our best interests, you haven't heard anything yet.

Stop Sitting On Your Arse Feeling Sorry For Yourself

I left Frank after eighteen months when I was seventeen and a half. I'm sure he didn't miss me, and I certainly didn't miss the hours and hours of graft I had to put in on those building sites for him. From that day to this, I've never worked for anyone but myself. I never will. But working for yourself brings its own challenges, problems and crises. I soon learned that the only person who can deal with them is you.

I was driving a car home from an auction in the early days when it conked out by the side of the motorway. I didn't know what to do. Every penny I had was invested in that car. As I sat by the side of the road, a hundred other cars must have zoomed past me. Not one of them stopped to help. I realised that there was no use sitting around on my arse feeling sorry for myself. I needed to get my dad to give me a tow back home, get the car cleaned up, fixed up and sold. Which is what I did.

I had to remember that incident in the early days of the Bank of Dave. Everywhere I turned, doors closed in my face. Everyone I spoke to presented me with problems rather than solutions. And maybe, if I hadn't learned the lesson that nothing ever gets done when you sit around feeling sorry for yourself, the whole project would have fizzled out before it had even begun.

Every business in the world runs into problems. When you're the person in charge, you soon learn that there aren't a whole load of people out there willing to lend a hand to fix things. As soon as you accept that, the world starts to make a bit more sense. You need to learn to sort things out for yourself, because like those drivers zooming past me on the motorway, nobody else is going to stop and help.

Spot Your Opportunities And Never Squander Your Stake

When I was about 21, I got myself a little garage in Nelson – not much more than a small forecourt and a Portakabin in the corner where I could do the paperwork. And in those early days, it was all about cars. I *liked* cars. There was something a bit trendy and sexy about them, and I enjoyed the thrill of being able to drive lots of different models and take something different home every night – anything from a Mini to a Rolls-Royce.

One day, though, I took a phone call from a guy who wanted to sell me a van: a red Astramax. I remember it like it was today. I remember thinking, what do I want a dirty old van for? But on a whim I thought: sod it, I'll give it a try. I bought this van – I think I gave £650 for it – and it was a right mess. I got in the back and started mucking out all the old cement – I had to crack it with a shovel first before I could even begin to shift it. It took a good day, maybe more, to scrub that thing clean, but I got it shining like any other car I'd put on the forecourt. Once it was cleaned up, I put it in *Auto Trader* magazine for sale.

The day the advert went in, my mobile phone went at half past five in the morning. In those days, it cost a fortune to call a mobile, so people always called the office number first. If someone was calling me at this hour, on this phone, it meant they *really* wanted to speak to me. I answered groggily, and heard a much chirpier voice at the other end. 'Hello? I'm ringing about the van.'

Van? What van? Then I remembered the Astramax.

'I'll have it!'

'But you haven't even seen it...'

'Don't matter. I'm on my way. Can you keep it?'

I jumped out of bed, got dressed, hurried to the garage and at seven o'clock the Astramax was sold.

Ten minutes later, I took another phone call. 'I'm ringing about the van.'

And ten minutes later, another.

All day: 'Van!' 'Van!' 'Van!'

Vans. It was a eureka moment. Life-changing. Forget the cars. Vans were where it was at.

Back then, twenty-odd years ago, vans were predominantly sold from farmyards, places where you'd need to stick on a pair of wellies to go and look at it and where the vehicles themselves were covered in shit and cement. People would buy them whatever condition they were in. There were no fancy showrooms or slick salesmen, and there were never more than three pages of them in *Auto Trader*. Now there are fifty or sixty.

The next day I was out there, looking for vans, buying up as many as I could possibly afford. I got rid of most of the cars and put all the money I had into vans. Whatever van I got my hands on, it sold straightaway. This was the beginning of the boom. The world and his wife were starting up businesses or working for themselves and needed a van to move their stuff around. People would come in looking for a Transit and walk out with something half the size of what they really wanted; they'd buy vans with dents in the side; they'd buy vans whose paint was still sticky where I'd had them resprayed overnight. It never stopped. Day in, day out. Week in, week out. Year in, year out. If a customer wanted to come along at midnight to buy a van, I was open for him. Even the guy at the local corner shop that was open all hours thought I was mad. But if someone was working seven days a week and could only come during his down hours, I had to be there to sell to him.

It was through the sale of vans that I build up my stake – the core capital I had with which to do business. When you're buying and selling, nothing is more important than your stake. It's like a monkey wrench to a plumber. Without it, you can't do anything. My stake started off as the £27 profit I made from the sale of my first car, but I never spent it. Instead I had a second job at night so I could bring in enough money to eat, while ploughing all my tiny profits back into my little business. Once I'd cobbled enough twenty-seven pounds together, I was able to get myself down the car auction. As my stake got bigger, so did my business. Now, I have millions of pounds worth of buildings and infrastructure and stock and I don't owe a penny to anybody. It all grew from that first twenty-seven quid, and I've only managed it because I've never squandered my stake. If anyone ever asks me about building up their stake, I always tell them that the first twenty grand is the hardest. If your stake is only a couple of grand and you've ploughed it into whatever product you're buying and selling, and then you see a bargain that you *know* will make you money, you can't buy it. Even if you know there's another thousand pounds profit sitting there waiting to be earned, if your stake's not big enough, you can't take advantage. And I always advise people that the best way to build up that first twenty grand is to get yourself a second job and squirrel away everything you earn. For most people, the day job pays for them to live, the evening job goes towards the stake. I did it the other way round, but however you choose to arrange your life, remember this: it's hard graft, but it pays dividends in the end. If you can earn yourself an extra £125 a week working three nights, it might not sound a lot. But when you multiply it by three years, it soon adds up to nearly twenty grand. And those three years won't be wasted. You can be planning what you want to do, performing your market research, preparing everything so that when your stake money is built up, you're ready to go. And in your mind, you'll know that you are moving towards something. You'll have a goal, you'll be on the path to attaining it. And trust me: the freedom that stake money will give you is priceless.

I was obsessed with my stake. Whenever I had a spare three or four grand, rather than go and buy myself a fancy car, I'd buy a house and rent it out. I've still got plenty of them today. (My first house cost me £4,200. I still own it. It's still rented out. Now it's worth £65,000.) So even when the vans were selling like hot cakes, and all my friends were mooching around in expensive cars, I was driving an ex-Transco van, because rather than spending my stake, I was building it up. I didn't care that people laughed at my old set of wheels. I knew what I was doing, and every day I jumped out of bed, totally focussed on building up that stake. I was convinced that if I got up early, focussed and set myself a goal to work towards, I *would* get there.

And then, one day, I got another call. It was from a bloke I'd been buying vans from. 'I've got something a little bit different, Dave,' he said. 'Could you just nip up here and have a look at it?'

The vehicle in question was a little red Transit minibus. He couldn't sell it and wanted me to take it off his hands. But what on earth did I know about minibuses? I wasn't impressed, but in the end he twisted my arm and I thought I'd give it a go. I took it back to the garage, scrubbed it up – all seventeen seats of it – then put it on my pitch and in *Auto Trader*.

Guess what. First thing next morning I was woken up by my mobile phone. 'The bus! I'll have it!'

Eureka!

That first minibus marked a turning point in my life. I went from that one bus to being the largest supplier of minibuses in the country.

And I didn't squander my stake. Every time I had some spare money, I bought another house, or more buses, or some land, or something tangible that would increase in value. I was in my early thirties before I started spending proper money on myself, but even then – and even now – I won't ever spend more in a week than I know I've earned. 'Don't spend what you haven't got' might sound like an obvious mantra, but I started investigating how our banks had got themselves into the mess they're in, I realised that this simple rule was something they had been flagrantly ignoring. When the time came to set up the Bank of Dave, I was adamant that I wouldn't fall into the trap of trying to spend what I hadn't got.

Surround Yourself With Good People

Did I mention that all businesses are about people? I meant it. The time soon came when I needed to bring in people to help me. I'd never employed anyone before, but I'd been on the other side of the fence during my time on the building sites. Without knowing it, I'd learned a lot about how to manage people, or perhaps more importantly how *not* to manage them. I remembered how hard I grafted, and for such a small amount that I never had any money left at the end of the week. I remembered Frank throwing his cap down on the floor in rage and screaming at me. In some ways I didn't really blame him, but I could certainly recall how that made me feel. And while I don't suppose he was all that desperate to keep hold of me as an employee, I couldn't help wondering if I would have been so eager to leave if he'd paid me a bit more and treated me a bit better. In a way, my philosophy of employing people was moulded on those building sites, and it hasn't changed since. Surround yourself with good people. As soon as you can afford to, pay them good wages – more than they'd get anywhere else. Look after them as if the shoe was on the other foot. Do these three things, and nobody will ever leave you.

People want to be respected and heard. If somebody in my organisation has a good idea, I listen to them. I empower them to take that idea forwards. A lot of the time they'll get it right, some of the time they'll get it wrong. Just like me – I get *loads* of things wrong. Just like anybody.

As I write this, there's a bright green minibus sitting on my forecourt designed by my right-hand man Mark. It will never sell as long as it stays bright green, but I'm not going to say that to Mark. At the same time, he's just designed – and sold – a bus based on an Aston Martin chassis with leather chairs and carbon fibre tables. It's beautiful. If Mark wants to buy a million pounds' worth of chassis tomorrow, he can do it. If he makes a mistake, we put it down to experience, but at the end of the day there's no doubt that the business is better for having him on board. I don't want to lose him, which means I need to make sure he doesn't want to lose me.

If someone's done a good job, I'm never afraid to tell them so. If they fuck up, I try not to dwell on it, because next time they have what might be a good idea, they'll remember getting a bollocking last time they used their initiative, and keep quiet.

So many people make the mistake of being invaluable. Of trying to be involved in every decision that's made. Of refusing to delegate responsibility. But one of the greatest secrets of running a successful business is to make yourself as *un*necessary as possible, as *quickly* as possible. In my several businesses we turn over millions of pounds a year, and my phone almost never rings. If I was an in-demand plumber, or ran a little cycle shop, my phone would never stop, and I'd be worried sick if it did. For me, it's the other way around. That doesn't mean I'm not in touch with what's going on in the businesses; it just means that I implicitly trust the people I've put in place to take care of things for me, and I've empowered them to make the decisions they need to make. This is not just a question of making your life easier. Most people are stuck inside the box spinning the plates and they can't see the woods for the trees. They need to step outside the box, stand on the edge and see what's going wrong. Then they can jump back in, fix it and maybe move on to a new business, or even four or five. If you're blinded by details, this is almost impossible to achieve.

There's a caveat to this, and it's an important one. Always make sure you can personally do every single job that's required in your business. Never rely on somebody else having to do something in the business that you can't do. It's years since I last scrubbed a minibus clean, but I know how to do it. I can silver the wheels and black the tyres. I can fix the vehicles. I can buy them. I can sell them. There's nobody in my business that I couldn't give their marching orders to because I'd be too worried that the firm would suffer. It's not that I don't appreciate the people I have, or that I don't want to keep them. I do. I'm proud of each and every one of them; I know how hard they work and I know how good they are. But for everyone's sake, not just mine, it's important that no single person becomes bigger than the business itself. So if somebody is doing a part of your business that you don't understand, get yourself clued up.

Know Where The Money's Going

There is one exception that proves the rule. The only responsibility that I never, ever delegate to anybody else is the signing of cheques. The reason is simple: I know that nobody, no matter how much I trust them, will spend my money the way I'd spend it. Nobody's going to focus on the bit in the middle the way I would. It doesn't matter if somebody has ordered £3.50 worth of stationery or a million pounds' worth of new vehicles: I look at the bill, I know who's ordered it and I sign the cheque myself. That way, I know where the money's going. I know whether we've paid the right price for that stapler or that consignment of vehicles. If I think we haven't, I put the bill to one side, have a word with the person responsible and give them a chance to go away and fix it. If they make the same mistake again, a bollocking might be in order. If not, they've taken on board what you've said. But if you'd let them sign the cheque in the first place, you'd never have known there was a problem, and it wouldn't take long for the bit in the middle to start feeling the squeeze. If you let other people spend your business's money, you won't have a business for very much longer.

This is such an important rule of business that it always surprises me when it's broken. How often do we read about a 'rogue trader' who has 'accidentally' gambled millions of pounds of a bank's money – which is to say, *your* money – on a deal that's gone pear-shaped? I've never deviated from this rule in all my business career, and I knew from the start that any speculating done by the Bank of Dave would be done by me. That way, the right person would carry the can if things went horribly wrong.

Know Your Business Inside Out

You need to understand every single thing about your business. It's only then that you'll be in a position to make changes for the better. If I didn't know everything about the minibus business, I wouldn't have made the success of it that I have. And if you think about starting your own enterprise, you need to bear that in mind. Let's say you want to open a pub. How would you go about it? What would you do?

Well, I'm sure you could enrol at your local college and do a diploma in something-or-other-to-do-with-pubs. It'll most likely take you a few years, you'll spend all your time looking at the inside of a classroom rather than the inside of the Dog and Duck and, worst of all, you'll probably be taught by people with lots of lovely business qualifications who've only ever seen the customer's side of the bar. It seems almost comical to me that our colleges and schools are full of business teachers who've never run a business. It's like me trying to get a pilot's licence at Blackpool airport with an instructor who tells me, 'I've never actually flown a plane before, but I've read the books!' It's madness and it needs to change: anyone teaching business should have a few years' successful experience, because there's no substitute for learning how to do business other than by doing business.

So, first things first: get yourself a job down your local. Do everything there is to do there. Change barrels, work the till, serve drinks, serve food, chat to the customers. You don't need to do it for a lifetime – a couple of months will be fine – but you do need to keep your eyes and ears open. Learn where the beer comes from. Learn where the best deals are to be had. Find out what the customers want.

When you've done that, go and have a look at what your competitors are doing. Go and sit in the nearest rival and drink tea all day long, well past the point where you've become a nuisance. And watch. How many people come in? How many go out? What do they order? What do they *want*? Speak to the customers about what they would like and what would persuade them to come into *your* pub. Are the owners putting on quiz nights? Do they draw a crowd? What sort of meat do they serve at Sunday lunch? How's the pub decorated? If it's one of the big chains you can bet your boots they'll have spent a fortune on interior designers and consultants decking the place out in such a way as to make people spend as much money as possible. That's money you don't have to spend: all you have to do is copy them. Or at least, copy the things that you think are working, and ignore the things that aren't. Be on top of what they're doing. In business, it always pays to keep your friends close, but your competitors closer. Don't try to reinvent the wheel; just try to do what your competitors are doing, only better. If they're offering carveries at £3.99, offer yours at £3.95. Sell off-peak dinners at £3.50 – remember you're paying rent and rates even when you're shut, and you're better off having a bit of something than nothing of nothing. Take the best ideas away and add your own.

And remember this. There are people out there who try to reinvent the wheel. Some of them do. Fantastic. The vast majority don't. You've a much better chance of success if you don't try to reinvent the wheel, but try instead to make a better one, or just sell it better. I had to keep this in mind in my quest to start my own bank. I wasn't going to reinvent banking. I wasn't going to be doing anything too much different to the big banks. I certainly couldn't be bigger, but I could try to be better.

Reverse Engineer Your Life

I've come a long way since I bought that first car back in the days when I was still working on the building sites. Things have changed. I'm no longer feeling my way through business, learning from my mistakes, working out what to do as I go along. Now it's different. Now people come to me asking for advice. I can understand why. You're too soon old and too late smart, and anyone who can help you get smarter earlier can improve your life immeasurably. When I look back over my career in business, I find myself wishing that there had been somebody to put their arm round me and say, 'Dave, don't do it like that, do it like this...'

So when people ask me for advice, I'm happy to oblige. And the one piece of advice I find myself giving more often than any other is this: if you want to succeed, you need to reverse engineer your life.

When I was starting out, I used to put photographs and cut-outs of things I wanted on the office wall, just behind my swivel chair. I'd have pictures of boats and sports cars and fancy houses. Whenever I started feeling the strain of keeping my little business going, I would spin round in my chair and give myself an eyeful of one of those boats. That quick reminder of how much I fancied one of them was enough to give me the focus I needed to crack on. There's an important lesson in there. I'm not saying everyone needs to stick a picture of a Sunseeker yacht or a Ferrari behind their desk, but they do always need to remember why they're doing what they're doing.

I sometimes go into schools and colleges, youth clubs or even businesses that have lost their way a little bit, and I ask the people I'm talking to one simple question. Where do you want to be in ten years' time, or fifteen years' time, or even twenty years' time? Do you want to be a millionaire? Do you want to own your own house? Do you want to work for yourself? It doesn't matter to me *what* their goal is; it doesn't even have to be financial. Maybe you want to write a book, or learn how to speak Spanish, or grow enormous prize-winning onions down your allotment, or retire at forty-five. What's important is that you *have* a goal, as there's no point blundering through life without knowing which direction you're travelling in.

So let's say you want to be a millionaire. That's your specific goal. Your aim. Your *raison d'être*. Fine. Get out your cheque book. It has to be a current cheque book, mind, drawing money on an actual bank account. This is real life. We're not playing around. Now, write yourself a cheque for £1 million. Sign it. Tear it out of the cheque book. Look at it. Feel pleased with yourself. You've achieved your goal already. All you've got to do now is find a way to make that cheque clear. Your goal is sorted. You've focussed your mind. You have a destination. The GPS is set. Press go.

Don't forget about that cheque. Put it somewhere very safe, but somewhere you can easily get to it – because from time to time you will need to take it out and look at it. Whenever you feel you're losing track, whenever your mind needs refocussing, take that cheque out of the drawer again. Look at it. Remind yourself of what it is you're doing. And be positive: you've already won the ovarian lottery by being born in the first place!

Believe me: it works. I can't promise you that you'll *become* a millionaire, or learn Spanish, or grow the biggest onions this side of Accrington. That's up to you. But I *can* promise you that if you don't stay focussed, you'll fail, and that keeping your eye on the prize is the best way to stay focussed. If you don't set yourself a destination, you won't know when you've got there. When you *do* get there, you can start rearranging your life so that you can make your way towards your *next* goal.

And remember this: the world's a big place, and your destination might be a long way off. But every journey starts with a single step. Only when you know where you're going do you know the direction in which that first step needs to be taken.

So that's the world according to Dave. There's nothing complicated about the way I go about things. Quite the opposite. I like things to be down to earth and unpretentious. That's how I've achieved whatever success is mine to lay claim to. Now that you know a bit about me, you've probably twigged that I'm not a saint. The business in which I've made my fortune isn't one for shrinking violets and Sunday School teachers, and I'm neither of them. Try and do a deal with me and I'll haggle you down to the very last penny. I'm fair, but in business I'm tough. There have been times in my past when someone going back on a deal has led to fist fights, and I've taken so many punches in my time that now I'm not scared of anything or anybody. In my world, everything is done on a handshake. If someone shakes on a deal and then goes back on it, their name is mud. To me, a handshake and your word is worth ten times more than a contract. If someone owes me money, then they owe me money. No two ways about it. But it works both ways: if I owe *you* money, I'd rather chop my left leg off than go back on my word.

What's more, I'm a businessman, not a charity. I'm not a fan of handouts, or of people getting something for nothing. I'm a fan of hard graft, of rewarding those people who are willing to put in a day's work, rather than those who wait for someone to come and dig them out of a hole. But that doesn't mean I'm not sympathetic to the situation some people find themselves in. I know what it's like to be poor. I know what it's like to struggle. I know what it's like when people won't give you a helping hand.

There's one more thing to add, and to my mind it's something that anyone who wants to make a few quid, or already *has* made a few quid, would do well to remember.

I'm not the wealthiest man in the world. I'm probably not even the wealthiest man in Burnley (although maybe I am).

But one thing's for sure: if that kid who started out all those years ago had been able to fast forward twenty years, he'd have thought that all his dreams had come true. In a way they have. But you soon learn that achieving your dream is not always everything you expect it to be. The top of a mountain can be a lonely old place; maybe that's why we're always looking for another peak to climb. And why is that? Simple. It's because you can only eat one breakfast, one dinner and one tea in a day. I eat the same cornflakes as everybody else. I watch the same programmes on the telly. I listen to the same music. For 95% of the day, having a lot of money makes no difference to having just enough. Don't get me wrong: I'd rather be able to pay my way than not, and I know how difficult it is for those that can't. Money gives you choices, but it doesn't solve all your problems. In fact, it gives you a whole set of *new* problems to worry about. I'm not trying to say I've got it hard these days, just that life is not an endless glass of champagne. And for me to stay motivated, I need to find something a little bit more worthwhile than the relentless accumulation of wealth.

When I was young, I was like a man possessed. Money was the only thing that was important to me and I pursued that goal with hardly a thought for anything or anybody else. I once saw an English businessman on the telly in a fancy penthouse suite in Las Vegas, drinking champagne in a big bubble bath. Now that, I thought to myself, looked like the life. He'd made it and one day, I decided, I was going to do the same thing. I went to Vegas several times over the next few years, seduced by the glitz and the glamour and the larger-than-life nature of the place. But I never stayed in that hotel room, and it was always an item on my list that I wanted to tick off. On one of my trips, I enquired about it. For the few days I wanted to stay there, it would cost $60,000. I negotiated it down to $25,000, which is still silly money in anyone's book, but for some reason I'd set my heart on it. I was young and daft, and I feel like a dick even talking about it nowadays, but I booked it.

My wife Nicky and I were given a gold card which we stuck in the elevator and it took us up to the penthouse. We felt special already. Our own butler was waiting for us, and a suite of rooms within rooms, each with a TV screen the size of Brierfield cinema that I used to go to as a kid. There were beds everywhere, and a jacuzzi; a steam room, a sauna and a private gym. I've really made it now, I thought to myself as I bounced up and down on one of the beds, looking out of the window over the amazing skyline of Las Vegas.

Time to make use of the exclusive facilities. I stuck my shorts on and had a go on the running machine. Had five minutes in the steam room. Five minutes in the sauna. Got the bubble bath going. Five minutes in there. Got dried, sat down, put one of the big tellies on, and said out loud...

'Shit.'

'What?' Nicky asked.

'I've been a dick.'

'Why? What's wrong?' She looked really concerned.

I shook my head. I'd just paid twenty-five thousand dollars to stay here. We had a telly in each room, I'd had a go in the sauna, I'd had a go in the jacuzzi, and the steam room, and the gym. I was bored with all that now. We'd come to Vegas, and what do you do in Vegas? If you're not asleep, you're out. You don't spend time in your hotel room. I'd just flushed twenty-five grand down the pan buying a few nights in a room I was already bored with and that I was hardly going to see. What a knob.

From that day to this, I've never wasted money like that because I learned the difference between the price of something and its value. If a can of Coke costs a pound, I'll pay; if it costs a fiver, I'd rather go thirsty. It's not that I can't afford it, it's just that I haven't forgotten the value of money.

Nowadays, things other than money drive me, and rightly so. I don't need a bigger house – there are only two of us living in our home and it's already like living in a hotel. We have to make a phone call to see if the other person fancies a brew if we're at opposite ends of the house. If I need a bigger place, something's wrong with me. I don't need a bigger helicopter – mine's already got four seats. There are some pictures taken of me a few years back in the days when I owned two Ferraris. It was ridiculous. Nicky and I had one each, like his and hers towels. And I remember looking at those photos and, instead of feeling pleased with myself and what I'd acquired, thinking: what a complete idiot. What the *fuck* have I got two Ferraris for, when they only get used once a week, if that?

I think there are too many people out there who wouldn't see very much wrong with having two Ferraris parked next to each other in their garage, or paying twenty-five thousand dollars for an expensive bubble bath in a Vegas hotel room. A lot of these people forget that their own wealth is based not only on their hard work, but also on the hard work of others. People like this see nothing wrong with collecting expensive trinkets that they don't really need, rather than using their wealth to give something back to the society that has enriched them so fabulously. My sneaking suspicion is that the industry where this attitude is prevalent is the banking industry. Why? Because it's the one industry that is *only* about making money, and nothing else. I don't believe the big banks think for a single second that they have any responsibility to share their good fortune. And I can't help wondering whether, if they stopped for just a moment to consider the communities around the country – around the *world* – that might benefit from just the tiniest change in attitude, it would give even the greediest and most grasping of that greedy, grasping bunch a small pause for thought.

THE BORING BIT

(or How to Make a Financial Weapon of Mass Destruction)

My wife Nicky reckons this is the boring bit of the book. Maybe she's right (she normally is). But then, she *is* used to listening to me bang on about things all day long; and she's *definitely* used to hearing me ask the question I'm going to try to answer in the next few pages. How the bloody hell can *anyone* lose themselves fifty billion quid?

It's easy to understand how most businesses make money because there's a product at the end of it. For me to make profit, I need to build a bus. I might have to fit wheelchair lifts or extra seats. There is a lot of work involved before I can get to the point of being able to *sell* it. All the banks seem to do is turn a £10 note into a £20 note. They're not actually making or producing anything. They just sell money for more money. How does that work? And how can they have lost all these billions? In this chapter I'm going to try to explain what they are *supposed* to do and what they *have* done. I'm not going to use fancy language or jargon nobody understands. Just a straightforward, no-bullshit walk through the world of banking. If that sounds boring, fair dos — I'll see you in the next chapter!

In the converted barn to the side of my property, I keep my own helicopter. Flying has been my passion for a number of years, and when the stresses and strains of taking care of my various businesses start building up, one of my favourite ways to relax is to take the helicopter out and go up to two or three thousand feet and sit on a cloud. I pick out the fluffiest one I can from the ground, then head up towards and through it. As I peek above the top, I lower my speed so I'm travelling at the same speed as the wind is blowing the cloud, clearing my mind and taking in the view before auto-rotating back down through the cloud with my eyes up towards the sky. There's nothing more peaceful or relaxing. Flying isn't without its dangers. I've had enough close calls behind the controls of my helicopter, and known enough pilots of my own calibre be involved in fatal accidents (of all my flying friends, 20 per cent have died in accidents), to realise that. But it's the only thing that floats my boat.

You're probably wondering what this has got to do with banks. Imagine you are sitting next to me in my helicopter and we're flying over a vast stretch of open water. The aircraft develops a problem; smoke starts billowing from the engines. We're going down. In the distance ahead of us, we can see two islands. We are miles from anywhere and nobody knows we're here. It's clear to us that we'll never be rescued from either island, but we have to make a decision which one to crash land on.

Happily, we remembered to bring an extra-powerful pair of binoculars. Using these, we can see that the island to our left is deserted, but covered with cases full of money. There must be billions of pounds just sitting there with nobody to claim it. But that's all there is. Just money. We turn our attention to the island to our right. There's no money here. There are, however, fields and livestock and fresh water. There are forests for wood and people working the land.

Which island do you suggest we head for? I hope it's the one on the right, because I'm the pilot and that's where I'm going.

The point is this: money, by itself, is worthless. You can't eat it. You can't build houses out of it. I suppose you could burn paper money to keep warm, but when it's gone, it's gone. It's only worth something when it can be exchanged in the future for goods or services. These are things of real value: the food that keeps us alive, the fuel that keeps us warm, the transport that allows us to move around. Money isn't much more than a way of allowing us to exchange these goods and services for *other* goods and services.

Let's imagine, for a moment, a world *without* any money. Let's also imagine that you have a Ford Fiesta and you want to swap it for a Rolls-Royce. How are you going to go about it? Well, you could scour *Auto Trader* in search of someone who's looking to swap their Rolls-Royce for a Ford Fiesta. Reckon you're going to find one? Me neither. What you might find, though, is someone who wants to get their hands on a Fiesta, and *another* person who wants to get rid of a Roller. Now we're getting somewhere, but how are we actually going to make the trade? Clearly we need something of value that you're prepared to accept for the Fiesta, and the fella with the big cigar and sheepskin coat is prepared to accept for his Rolls-Royce. Something that is *always* acceptable in any trade of goods or services. That 'thing of value', of course, is money.

Our currency doesn't *have* to be cash as we know it, of course. The system of notes and coins that we use today is quite a recent invention. Throughout history, all sorts of objects have been used instead, from cattle to salt. The idea of swapping a herd of cows for your Fiesta might sound strange, but in some ways it makes sense because cows are actually useful: you can milk them, you can eat them, you can make shoes out of them. And if your buyer throws in a bag of salt, you can make your steak taste better too. There's nothing inherently valuable about a five-pound note. It's only worth something because we all agree that it is. And it has obvious advantages over cows and salt. If salt were our currency, you could become a millionaire by swiping a few buckets of seawater; it's not quite so easy to start printing your own tenners. And if you didn't spend your cows, you'd be pretty miffed when they died on you after a couple of years.

The point is this: money is only worth something because we say it is, and we all have to agree on its value if it's going to be useful. Historically, the value of paper money was always linked to the value of gold. You could, in theory, exchange your money at any time for the quantity of gold it represented. Not, of course, that there's anything inherently valuable about gold either; we just *think* it's valuable because it's scarce and pretty. It is also useful as a currency because it's hard to counterfeit and is fairly easy to lug around. This system of paper money being backed up by quantities of gold is known as the gold standard. Britain left the gold standard in 1931; America continued with a version of it for another forty years. Now, our paper money and coins are not backed up by gold, but by trust. We *trust* that everyone is going to agree on the value of money. We *trust* that people are going to use it as though it really were backed up by something of value that we can touch. When that trust gets betrayed, the results – as we've all witnessed – can be cataclysmic.

So, put like this, we can see that money is nothing more than barter. A way of keeping score. And if we go back to our quest for a new car, we'll soon find out that nobody really wants to swap a Rolls-Royce for a Fiesta, but as we all agree on the value of our currency – pounds sterling – this isn't a problem. We just need to add some more money to the pot we have from the sale of our Fiesta, hand it over to the Rolls-Royce owner, and drive away in our new Silver Shadow. If everything has gone well, all three people involved in the transaction feel like they've come away with something they wanted. Something useful. Something valuable. Everyone's a winner.

So that's what money is. Sounds obvious, doesn't it? We all have things we want to swap with other people – food, clothes, cars, our own time and labour – and we need some standard way of keeping tabs on what we've swapped and with whom. So we invent money. But the money, crucially, isn't a thing of value in itself: it represents, and gets exchanged for, actual things.

Except, of course, that isn't always true. Not any more. The reason being that, at the same time as history was inventing money, it was also inventing bankers.

Let's get one thing straight: banks are important. Why? Because when they do what they're supposed to do, they're more than just an alternative to sticking your wages under the mattress. In a world where everybody wants to trade with everybody else, they do something that's absolutely fundamental: they lend money. If we're going to understand how the banking crisis happened, we need to understand why they lend money, and how it all started. So let's imagine our own little bank in our own little universe. We'll call it Barry's Bank.

Barry's Bank is set up by Barry the Banker in a world where there is no paper money, and all transactions are carried out in gold. It's a simple place: just a room with a safe. Barry the Banker's business plan is as simple as his premises. He'll look after people's gold for them in the safe, and he'll pay them interest – a little bit more gold, to add to their stash. The longer they keep their gold in the safe, the more interest they'll earn. Any time they want to take some or all of their gold out, they just have to ask. This seems like a very good deal to his customers. They can put their money somewhere very safe and, in addition, they can make it work for them. They don't think too hard about *how* Barry the Banker is managing to pay them this interest.

So how *does* he? He lends the gold in his safe to other people, and charges them a small fee – a little extra gold – for the service. He can do this because it's not very likely that all his depositors will ask for all their money at the same time. The fees he earns from lending, minus the interest he pays his depositor, minus his overheads, is his profit – his bit in the middle.

Like I said, it's a very simple setup, but in order for everything to run smoothly, certain things have to happen:

1. The borrowers have to repay the interest on their loans, and the loan itself, when they're supposed to.
2. There needs to be enough gold in the bank for the depositors to make small withdrawals whenever they want to.
3. The banker needs to be sure that a situation won't arise where all the depositors want to take all their gold out at once, because there won't be enough in the safe. (Do the words 'Northern Rock' ring a bell?)

*

If Barry the Banker is careful, none of these should be a problem and he's got himself a nice little business. Everyone's happy: the depositors earn interest, the borrowers can fund whatever they need to fund, and Barry makes an honest profit. He also makes quite an *easy* profit. He doesn't have to *make* anything, or *supply* anything, or even provide much of a *service*. As long as he charges more to lend money than he pays in interest, and his three golden rules are adhered to, he has to try pretty hard to *fail* to make a profit. But we shouldn't forget that there's a little sleight of hand going on here. Barry the Banker's depositors *think* that all their gold is sitting in his safe. This isn't true. In fact, only a small fraction of the gold is there.

Let's think for a minute about one of the people borrowing gold from Barry's Bank. We'll imagine that he makes tables, and we'll call him Colin the Carpenter. Now, Colin the Carpenter has a problem. Loads of people want to buy his tables, but he can't work fast enough to make all the tables he could sell. If only he could employ somebody to take over the time-consuming job of varnishing the tables for him. That way, he could increase his production. But there's not a lot of money in table-making, and the little profit he makes isn't enough to take on somebody else: he simply wouldn't be able to pay them. However, if Barry the Banker could lend him some of the gold in his safe – just enough to cover a few months' wages for an extra person – Colin the Carpenter would be able to sell more tables, and earn enough money to pay off the loan. And when the loan is paid off, he'll have enough to keep paying his new member of staff, and maybe take home a little bit more gold for himself.

Put like this, we can see that Barry's Bank lending gold isn't just a way of making Barry and his depositors rich. It has helped to expand a business; it has helped give another person a job; and if Colin the Carpenter does take home a bit more gold, perhaps he'll buy his missus a bunch of flowers now and then, which will really help Fanny the Florist down the road. Who knows – maybe *she'll* be able to take on an extra member of staff fairly soon, too. Employment starts to boom. Barry's Bank might be based on a little deception but it has become, by anyone's standards, a force for good.

Of course, Barry the Banker has to be careful. Colin the Carpenter *thinks* he can sell more tables, but it's not a guarantee – and this is Barry's depositors' money he's lending out, after all. So, he checks Colin is on the level. He visits him. He looks into the man's eyes and satisfies himself that he's trustworthy. And then they make a deal: if Colin the Carpenter can't pay back his loan, Barry the Banker will be able to take the wood from his warehouse and sell it to cover his losses. But he certainly doesn't *want* to do that. He's in the banking business, not the wood-selling business. Going down that route would be nothing but hassle. If he's smart, he'll do everything he can to help Colin's business along. Perhaps he can give him a bit of advice on how to get overheads down; maybe one of his other clients sells chisels and can do him a deal. It's in everyone's interests for Barry the Banker and Colin the Carpenter to have a good and constructive relationship.

Barry is doing very well out of his little banking business. But like most business-owners, he'd like it to grow. One way of doing this would be to attract more depositors, and to lend more money. Now that he's found his feet, however, he's beginning to think that there might be a sneakier way to increase his bottom line. It occurs to him that rather than hand out actual gold when somebody takes a loan from him, he could simply write out promissory notes which *represent* the gold. If anyone comes into his bank and returns one of these notes, Barry the Banker will immediately exchange it for the amount of gold it represents. He has, in fact, just invented paper money. To start with – and this is very important – the amount of paper money Barry's Bank circulates is backed up by exactly the same value of actual gold in his safe. If somebody has a note representing ten nuggets of gold, they can go to Barry's Bank, look in the safe, and see the actual gold there. If they want to swap the notes for the gold, they can.

It doesn't take long to dawn on Barry, however, that he could do something quite crafty. It never seems to happen that everybody who owns one of his notes comes in at the same time to demand the gold it represents. He realises that there's nothing to stop him issuing more notes than he has gold to back them up. As long as everybody doesn't turn up at the same time, Barry the Banker can lend more money than he actually has, earn more interest, make more profit – and nobody will be any the wiser.

Barry puts his plan into action and it works like a dream. He starts to grow very wealthy indeed. It seems that more and more people want loans and they want them for all kinds of things: to expand their businesses, to buy houses, to buy vehicles. He produces more and more notes. The more he produces and lends out, the more interest he earns.

But you can probably see a problem here. The more notes he produces, the smaller the proportion of them that is backed up by actual gold in his safe. To build up his gold reserves, Barry the Banker persuades more people to deposit their gold in his bank, but even so, after a while, he has issued several times the amount of notes compared to his stash of gold.

I think it's safe to imagine that people would start to notice Barry's wealth. They smell a rat. What has he been doing with that gold of theirs? Are his bank notes really as valuable as they thought? If enough people smelled enough rats, chances are that the one thing Barry doesn't want to happen, *does* happen. They all turn up on the doorstep of Barry's Bank one day, demanding their gold. (Northern Rock ring a bell again?)

And Barry hasn't got enough to pay them. He's been found out.

This is where the government of our imaginary universe comes in. What do they do with Barry the Banker? Sling him in prison? Close down Barry's Bank? Stop anyone else from ever doing the same thing again?

Well, they *could*. But there's another problem. No matter what everybody might think of what Barry the Banker has done, one fact is unavoidable. Because Barry the Banker has been lending money, Colin the Carpenter now employs a team of twenty people, and all of them buy their wives and girlfriends a bunch of flowers every week, which means Fanny the Florist has moved to bigger premises and employs five flower arrangers. They've all taken out mortgages with Barry's

Bank to buy houses, which has kept three construction businesses, each employing a hundred people, busy for years. The bottom line is that everybody needs Barry's Bank to keep ticking over. And so, rather than stamp on Barry the Banker, they do the exact opposite: they make what he has been doing perfectly legal, and encourage him to keep doing it.

They do put some restraints on him. They call it regulation. They tell him that he's only allowed to lend, say, nine times as many notes as he actually has gold deposits to back it up with. So, for every gold coin he has, he can lend nine notes. That way, they hope, they can stop things spiralling out of control. The government is fairly relaxed about Barry growing very rich, but there's a flip side to the deal: he *has* to lend to the businesses and the people who need loans.

He *has* to lend money. It's the only reason he's allowed to carry on.

So he does. Soon, the tiny amount of gold in his safe is irrelevant. All that matters is the paper money, and Barry the Banker is allowed, quite literally, to make it.

Still with me? Good – we're a little bit closer to understanding how Barry and his banker mates fucked things up for the rest of us.

Let's imagine starting a new bank from scratch, a bank regulated in the way we've just talked about. Our new bank doesn't work with gold, but with pounds sterling, and because it only has to have a fraction of the money it lends actually sitting in its safe, it is called a Fractional Reserve bank.

Our bank will have certain start-up costs. We'll need to buy a building, for example, and a safe. So before we can do anything, we will need to put up some money to cover this, say £100. We'll call this £100 our equity, and represent it in a picture like this.

Assets	Liabilities	Equity
		£100

Having spent a hundred quid on a building and safe, our bank now has some assets, worth £100.

Assets	Liabilities	Equity
Building and Safe		**£100**

On the day our bank opens, a horde of customers turns up, each wanting to deposit their money with us and take advantage of our 5% interest rate. Between them, they deposit £1,000. This £1,000 is a liability for our bank, because our customers can turn up and ask for it back at any time. They have, in effect, lent it to us; we therefore owe it to them. Let's add it to our picture.

Assets	Liabilities	Equity
	£1,000 deposit	
Building and Safe		**£100**

In order to be able to pay our 5% interest, we need to make this money work for us, which means lending it out. We can't lend it all out, because there needs to be enough money for some of our depositors to remove some of their funds at any given time. So we leave £100 in the bank, which we will call our reserve, and lend out £900 at an interest rate of 10%. The £100 cash and £900 of loans are assets for the bank, and we'll illustrate them like this

Assets	Liabilities	Equity
£900 loans	£1,000 deposit	
£100 reserve		
Building and Safe		£100

So far so good. Let's imagine nothing changes for a year. What will our balance sheet look like? How much have we earned and paid out? Our loans have brought in 10% of £900, which is £90. We've paid out 5% of £1,000 in interest, which is £50. Let's say that our overheads have been £10, and that we pay 20% tax on our profit.

Interest earned	£90
Interest paid	-£50
Overheads	-£10
Pre-tax profit	£30
Tax	-£6
Net profit	**£24**

So now, rather than having £100 in our cash reserve, we have £124; our equity has increased by £24 and our balance sheet looks like this.

Assets	Liabilities	Equity
£900 loans	£1,000 deposit	
£124 reserve		
Building and Safe		£124

Which looks to me like a good business.

Of course, in reality, things are a bit more complicated than this. Let's imagine that our £900 loan went to a construction firm to build a new road. What did the firm do with that money? They spent it, of course, on workers and materials. As we're the best bank around, the workers and suppliers deposit their earnings back in our bank. So now, our original balance sheet looks something like this.

Assets	Liabilities	Equity
	£900 deposit	
£900 loans	£1,000 deposit	
£100 reserve		
Building and Safe		£100

What are we going to do with this extra money? Well, we need to pay our new depositors some interest, so we need to lend it out. As before, we hold back a chunk in case any of our new depositors want to make a withdrawal. This will be 10%, or £90. The rest, we lend – perhaps to a company who wants to build some houses.

Assets	Liabilities	Equity
£810 loans	£900 deposit	
£90 reserve		
£900 loans	£1,000 deposit	
£124 reserve		
Building and Safe		£100

But hang on a second... Suddenly we're lending out a lot more than the initial £1,000 that we had at the beginning. Where has this new money *come* from? Well, you remember Barry the Banker? He was allowed, in the end, simply to *create* cash. That's what's happened here, and that's what happens with all our major banks. When somebody takes out a new loan, the money is conjured into existence with the tap of a computer.

By lending out, we've created wealth. It doesn't really matter that there's not enough actual cash to back it up, because most of the money is just moved from account to account, using cheques or bank transfers. Think of your own pay cheque. How much of that money do you ever actually *see* in cash? The wealth our bank has created represents debt rather than cash or gold, but it can still be used to buy goods and services.

But...

What happens if our road constructor and our house builder, for whatever reason, go bankrupt and cannot pay back their loans? Our bank has suddenly lost two of its major assets – they simply disappear – and the picture suddenly looks less rosy.

Assets	Liabilities	Equity
	£900 deposit	
£90 reserve	£1,000 deposit	
£100 reserve		
Building and Safe		£100

We have a building worth £100, plus £190 in cash reserves. But we owe our depositors £1,900. If they come in and ask for their money, we won't be able to give it to them. We've lost it. And that, of course, is a pretty big problem – not just for us, but for our depositors, because the debt backing up their money no longer exists. The numbers in their bank account are meaningless because we can't pay them back. The bank is no longer 'liquid'.

If a bank stops being liquid, it can borrow money from a 'reserve bank'. In the UK, this is the Bank of England. There is also an organisation called the Financial Services Compensation Scheme – a kind of insurance policy which guarantees all depositors' money up to £85,000 if the bank goes bust. But you have to wonder: if *you* were a bank, and you *knew* that the FSCS would pay up if things went pear-shaped, would that encourage you to invest safely but less profitably? Or might you be tempted to act recklessly and *more* profitably?

Let's recap. Banks use our money to create wealth. They are allowed to do this because, by lending money, they help businesses develop and, hopefully, keep the economy in a good state of health. When things go wrong, however, they can go very wrong indeed. And to see just *how* wrong they can go, we'll imagine that our bank decides to specialise in mortgages.

In theory, a mortgage should be a very safe loan for a bank. This is because the house against which the loan is taken out is offered as security against the money the homeowner has borrowed. If the borrower defaults, the bank can repossess the house and sell it to get its money back. So before giving a mortgage, a bank should work out how much the house in question would be worth if they had to sell it tomorrow. Its purchase price might be £100,000, but if it would only achieve £70,000 in a quick sale, the bank would be bloody daft to lend more than that sum. They should also think about whether the borrower can pay back the loan. If he or she takes home £1,000 a month, and the mortgage costs £800 a month, chances are they're going to come a cropper. But done properly, a mortgage is a safe loan, which is why the interest rates are lower than for usual loans.

So far, so straightforward. But perhaps you remember, not so long ago, that some of our high street banks started offering 105% loans. For our £100,000 house, this means that they would be lending £105,000 against a property that they might only be able to sell quickly for £70,000.

Perhaps the phrase 'sub-prime mortgage' also means something to you. It was bandied around all over the shop at the start of the financial crisis, but what does it actually mean? A sub-prime mortgage is a loan given to a borrower with a poor credit rating, somebody who is more likely to default on their loan and fail to pay the mortgage back. At the start of the crisis in America, 20% of mortgage loans were sub-prime.

Why would we, as banks, make loans like this? The reason is simple. If a borrower is classed as 'sub-prime', we can charge them a bit more for the mortgage and, hopefully, make a larger profit. And this is fine when times are good. Employment is high, our borrower has a job and he can make his monthly repayments. The housing market is booming. His property increases in value. If you don't look at it too hard, our sub-prime loan looks like a good investment.

But what happens when times become a bit harder? Our borrower loses his job and can't pay us back; the housing market falls and his house is worth a lot less than the money we've lent on it. He might even say, 'Fine, repossess it,' and walk away. Suddenly we've lost money. And if you multiply that one home loan by 100,000, suddenly we've lost a *lot* of money.

Sounds bad, right? Unfortunately, that's not the half of it.

Mortgages are debts. And as we've already seen, for a bank, debts are assets. They can package up a load of their dodgy home loans and sell them to an investment bank in the City. The investment bank then gets an organisation called a ratings agency to put an 'AAA rating' on this batch of mortgages. An AAA rating means that, in the opinion of the ratings agency, these are good loans.

But here's the thing. The bank *pays* the ratings agency to give the batch of mortgages a rating. This is like a car dealer paying one of his mates to look over a car, then go and tell the customer it's a good 'un. And maybe it *is* a good 'un. Or maybe the car dealer's mate thinks that this is a nice little earner, and it doesn't make any difference to *him* what he says about the car – it's more important that the dealer keeps coming to him, wallet in hand.

So, now we have a batch of dodgy mortgages with a dodgy rating sitting on the balance sheet of a fancy investment bank somewhere in the Square Mile. The scene is set for us to roll out the Financial Weapon of Mass Destruction that brought the economies of the world to their knees. It is called the Credit Default Swap.

Take that car you've just bought, and imagine buying some insurance for it. You pay an insurance company £150 a year, and if you have a crash, they'll pay you a chunk of money. Nothing wrong with that. How would you feel, though, if somebody else took out some insurance against you having a crash? Of course, in the world of car insurance that would never happen. The world of banking is different.

A Credit Default Swap is an insurance policy on a loan. The seller of the CDS agrees to pay out the value of a loan if it goes bad. But the buyer of the CDS doesn't have to be the person who owns the loan. In this situation, one side is betting that the loan is good; the other side is betting that it will go bad.

And here's the crazy bit. A bank that owns these dodgy mortgages can buy a CDS to insure themselves against them going bad, but also sell a CDS to another bank, effectively betting that the loans *won't* go bad. Imagine a complex network of Credit Default Swaps, bought and sold by all the commercial banks and investment banks in financial centres all over the world, and all centred around toxic, sub-prime loans with a bogus AAA rating. It's a house of cards. As soon as the loans start to go bad – and they will, because they are all based on mortgages worth more than the houses securing them – the whole thing tumbles down.

And this is what happened.

In a frighteningly short space of time, almost all the banks found themselves with no liquidity. Because of their reckless betting, their reserves were all dried up. They had no money to lend. They had no money to do *anything*.

They were bust.

Do you remember Colin the Carpenter, the table-maker that Barry the Banker lent money to at the beginning of this chapter? What if, all of a sudden, *he* went bust? It could happen for all sorts of reasons. Maybe there's a spate of forest fires and the price of wood goes through the roof. Maybe there's a new carpenter in town, making better tables for less money. What would happen? He'd have to lay off his staff and sell off his premises to pay back the bank the money he owes. Perhaps he can't raise it all and the bank takes a hit. Colin the Carpenter going out of business isn't great for anyone. He and his staff are out of work and Fanny the Florist will sell fewer flowers. It's bad news. But it's not a massive catastrophe. We can't imagine the government stepping in to stop it happening.

A bank going out of business is a different matter. For a start, it could have many millions of pounds' worth of customers' money on deposit. Even though, as we've seen, the Fractional Reserve banking system means they don't *actually* have that money in their safe, they still need sufficient cash reserves to be able to pay *some* of their customers *some* of their money at any given time. If these reserves were depleted, it would be bad enough. The government would end up having to pay back the depositors' money – expensive for all of us.

But no reserves also means no lending, and we know how important it is that banks should be lending. It's why they're allowed to do what they do in the first place.

When banks' reserves have dried up to the point that they stop lending, it's called a credit crunch. And it's a bloody disaster for everyone.

A TINY, TINY BANK

Let me introduce you to Big Roy, Burnley's jeweller-in-chief.

You could write on the back of a postage stamp what Big Roy doesn't know about buying and selling gold. As a young man, fresh out of university, Roy was offered a job down in the Channel Islands. While he was waiting for that job to start, he found himself a temporary position working in a factory in Blackburn, where he got to know a Polish fella who was selling watches. Roy had £500 savings. Rather than squander it, he decided to try and turn that £500 into £1,000 by buying some of these watches and then selling them on for a profit. It wouldn't happen immediately, he figured, but he was in no hurry.

His mum fell ill and was hospitalised. Roy stayed in Blackburn to be with her. By the time she recovered, he'd lost the job in the Channel Islands. He had no money. In fact he had nothing except his little consignment of watches which he needed to convert back into cash. Roy got himself a stall at Accrington market, where he laid his watches out on a table. They sold like hot cakes, and Roy had taken his first step on the path he would follow for the rest of his career. An elderly Jewish Orthodox gentleman called Benjamin Solomon took Roy under his wing. He'd been buying and selling not only watches but also precious metals from local people for many years. Roy learned the ropes of his trade from this old hand. He also learned the ethics of the trade: be fair with everybody, never pull the wool over their eyes and never, ever try to force people to sell items they may cherish.

Roy's shop, where today he buys and sells gold and silver trinkets and other items of value, is just a few doors along from the premises that would eventually become the Bank of Dave. It's the very opposite of Tiffany & Co. Small and unpretentious, there are a few glass cabinets displaying objects Roy thinks he might sell to the public; but the main tool of his trade is a small pair of scales on which he weighs items – normally gold and silver – that local people bring in to sell for whatever reason. Maybe they're on their uppers; maybe the item is surplus to requirements. Roy gives them a fair price compared to the value of gold or silver on that particular day. Then he'll either re-sell the object, or sell it for the metal price, in which case it will be melted down and recycled. Roy explained to me once that his humble little shop is an excellent barometer of how the economy is faring. He knew, a year before any politicians or bankers had even mentioned the possibility of the recent economic collapse, that something was in the wind. Local people were coming in selling jewellery and precious heirlooms simply to cover that month's standing order for their mortgage. Often Roy found himself writing out cheques not to the individual, but to their mortgage company. And it gave him no great pleasure to see this upturn in his own trade. These were local people encountering hardship, and Roy is a local person too. Their problems are his problems.

The other side of Roy's business – supplying jewellery – is a perfect example of a small business needing credit in order to thrive. If somebody wants to buy a diamond, Roy can source it for them, without any problem, from a diamond dealer. But diamonds are expensive and Roy isn't De Beers. It's not uncommon that he needs to borrow the funds to purchase the diamond in the first place, before selling it on at a small margin. It's a mainstay of his business, and without credit, his wings are clipped.

I'm sure Big Roy wouldn't mind me observing that he's not the type to take any shit from anyone. And if anyone was under the impression that the people worst affected by the banking crisis were the needy and defenceless, Roy'd soon put them right. Come into his store and try to rob him and he'd soon manhandle you back out on to the street, with his Alsatian at his side. And he'll not try to charm you. Get him talking about the banks and he'll give you his opinion in no uncertain terms: that they're not fit for purpose. Roy's a rough, tough man of the north, and absolutely not the kind of bloke you'd ever see begging some spotty, wet-behind-the-ears bank manager for credit. He's the first person to admit that there might have been times in the past when he's been late on his gas bill, or he's missed a payment for this, that or the other.

But that doesn't mean he's not a good, honest, ethical person. I remember sitting in Roy's shop when a young lad walked in with cuts on his face, stinking of booze and with needle marks up his arm that suggested alcohol wasn't his only vice. He was clutching a handful of jewellery and had a desperate look in his eyes. It would have been the easiest thing in the world for Roy to buy this lad's offerings at a fraction of the going rate so that he could get his next fix, but Roy wouldn't have anything to do with him. Even if the kid wasn't offering him stolen goods, it was obvious where any money Roy paid out would end up going. I wonder how many profit-at-any-cost bankers would be quite so choosy about where they made their money. I wonder if they'd even check. Roy has never taken a single penny in benefits from the government. There are no bailouts for him. And yet he has trouble borrowing money from the banks to conduct his business. He might have a buyer and seller lined up. It might be a done deal, but for the finance. And yet, of late, the doors have been closed to him.

I know Roy and I've known him for years. I know how he cares about his reputation. In his own words, 'My name's my name.' And I know that if I lend him money, he'll pay me back. And if the high street banks bothered to get their arses down to Roy's shop and spent the time getting to know him, if they asked around to see what local businessmen and customers had to say about him, rather than relying on a computer to estimate whether he's good for the money or not, I've no doubt they'd reach the same conclusion. But, of course, they would never do that.

In late 2008, early 2009, I found myself with a problem not unlike Roy's. My customers were coming to me wanting a new bus, just as they had done for the last twenty years. But new buses are expensive pieces of kit. They couldn't simply buy them outright. And so, just as they'd always done, they would decide to borrow the money. Once they'd chosen a bus, they'd fill in a finance form. So far, so normal.

The ordinary sequence of events would be this. The finance form would be faxed off to the bank or whatever financial institution was offering the loan; the loan would be approved and the bank would write me a cheque for the value of the bus or van; the customer would then have the vehicle delivered to them, or would come and pick it up. Simple. And for some time, the banks had been falling over themselves to issue these loans. When they realised that we were spreading our financing across a number of different banks and institutions, it started to get competitive. We had been able to pick and choose between those banks that were offering my customers the best deals. They were fighting for our business, and rightly so. My customers were decent, honest, ethical people. They were running their own businesses, and were fully aware that they needed to pay the money back or they would lose the bus. They would do everything in their power to stop this from happening, because these buses were their livelihoods. Perhaps they'd have a contract to take kids to school in the morning and drop them home in the afternoon; during the day they'd use the bus to do some airport runs; in the evenings they'd take folk on nights out to Blackpool. However they used them, the vehicles were the lifeblood of their businesses. They'd done the sums: they knew what they could earn from their bus, they knew what the loan costs were. They *weren't* going to risk losing it. And this was how it had been for as long as I'd been in the business.

Almost overnight, things changed. The finance forms started to be rejected. I couldn't understand why. My customers didn't start doing anything differently. They didn't suddenly stop being decent or honest or ethical. Loans that would definitely have been approved in the past were turned down. The banks and financial institutions had lowered the bar. They had gone from one extreme to another; from lending recklessly and indiscriminately to too many people, to refusing credit to people who truly needed credit in order to keep their modest shows on the road.

Hopefully, by now, you have some idea of why this happened. Quite simply, the banks had run out of money. This was their own fault. It was a direct result of their greed and recklessness in the past. A direct result of their using the concessions given them for the purpose of keeping the economy moving, to enrich themselves to an eye-watering degree. It was certainly not the fault of my customers. But it was my customers whose livelihoods, all of a sudden, were on the line. And my own business was facing a real danger. If people couldn't get credit, they couldn't buy buses. And if they couldn't buy buses, my business was looking over the precipice, and so were all the people I employed.

I had to make a decision very quickly. I had two options. Either my business took a massive hit, or I decided to do what the banks couldn't, or wouldn't, do: lend the money myself.

They say necessity is the mother of invention. Well, it was necessity that was driving me down this path. I wasn't a massive international bank. I didn't have billions at my disposal. You don't have to finance very many minibuses before you expose yourself to a substantial amount of risk if the loans go bad. But surely, I told myself, I could hardly bellyache about the banks turning my customers down if I was going to do the same thing. If I *truly* believed my customers were good for the money, what did I have to lose?

I approached it with a bit of common sense. I looked at the loan requests. Did the customers live where they said they lived? Yes. Were they buying what they said they were buying? Yes. Did I understand the product they were buying? Of course, I built it. Were the customers going to pay me? Why wouldn't they – they'd paid the banks and finance company on the nose for the last ten or fifteen years. Finally, and most importantly, could they afford it?

I took the decision to start lending. To this day not a single one of my business customers has failed to pay back their loan.

It didn't take me long to realise just how much the banks had been making out of me and my customers. I was the person who had been making the buses and employing all the people in my business; my customers were the people who were working hard all day to service the loans; yet the banks had been making more profit out of it than anyone –

more than me, and certainly more than my clients doing their school runs and taking old ladies to hospital.

But the banks hadn't *done* anything! They hadn't made anything. They hadn't got their hands dirty. So far as I could see, they had done nothing but take £10 and turn it into £20. And I asked myself this: what other business do I know that is too big to fail, that will be bailed out by the taxpayer if it gets into trouble, and can turn £10 into £20 by doing *absolutely nothing*? And how on *earth* could a business like that find itself £50 billion in the red? That was the figure I kept hearing. Sometimes it was a few billion more (but hey, what's a few billion between friends?). I read reports in the newspapers of bankers suffering crippling stress, burned out from the pressure of their jobs. On the same pages I was reading about soldiers in Afghanistan being shot at on a daily basis. I know who I thought was under the greater pressure, but the soldiers weren't earning hundreds of thousands of pounds for their trouble. It left a bad taste in my mouth.

I didn't have to lend to my customers forever – when money started easing back into the world, I was able to take my foot off the gas, although I did still offer to underwrite loans from the bank in order to make them keener to lend – but it was a good decision to start offering loans to my customers. My business continued to do well, even when others started to struggle through lack of credit. And then, one day in mid-2009, one of my four different bank managers came along to one of my offices in Burnley. I won't say which bank he represented, but it was one of the big four. If you haven't got a bank account with them, I guarantee you know somebody who does. We sat down together over a cup of tea, and he explained the reason for his visit.

'Right, David,' he said. 'We're going to lend you some money.'

I was pretty taken aback – not only because this seemed to be an about-turn, but also because I hadn't asked for a loan in the first place. 'I don't need any money,' I told him.

'I know you don't need any money,' the bank manager replied. 'But we're going to lend you some anyway.'

I still didn't understand. Maybe I was being thick. 'Why should I borrow any,' I asked, 'if I don't need any?'

The bank manager explained that he'd been given a certain amount of money by the government in the wake of the credit crisis, and they were obliged to lend it out. 'But I don't want to lend it to just anybody,' he said. 'Not if there's even the smallest possibility that they won't pay it back.'

I couldn't believe what I was hearing.

'I've picked my top customers,' he carried on, 'and you're one of them. I'll lend this money to you so cheaply that it won't be worth you *not* having it. Whatever you do with it, you'll make a profit. You could stick it back in the bank and make money. The government's told us we *have* to lend it out, but I only want to give it to people I *know* will pay it back. I only want to give it to people like *you*.'

To say I was shocked was like saying Fred the Shred should lose his knighthood. I thought of all my customers who couldn't get credit. All those people whose livelihoods were threatened by everything the banks had done. And I thought back to when I was starting out in the car business, to the garage owner who had first trusted me to take one of his part-exchange cars in the hope that I'd be able to sell it and bring him back his seventy quid. Everybody needs a leg-up sometimes, and that's what the banks were there to do. I thought of the billions of pounds that taxpayers had pumped into the banks just to stop them from going bust. These taxpayers weren't, in the main, rich bastards and high-flyers. They were honest, working-class members of the small communities that were now struggling so desperately because of the financial institutions their money had helped to save, and who were now hoping for a little bit of support in return.

And I told him exactly what I thought.

'You need to go out there,' I said, 'and lend that money to the people who really need it, because it could be a lifeline that could save their business. For me to take that money would be morally and ethically wrong and I'm not prepared to do it, not even if you give it to me for free. I'm going to forget this conversation ever took place. You need to walk out of that door and find the people you're *supposed* to be lending to.'

The subject was never mentioned again.

I've no doubt that the bank manager completely ignored me; no doubt that the money his bank had been given to help those struggling businesses who most needed it ended up in the accounts of people like me who absolutely did not need it. And I'm quite sure that he was not the only bank manager doing this. After everything the banks had done, all the misery and hardship they'd caused, and after every single person in the country had bailed them out, this was what they were up to.

It wasn't right. This was yet more proof to me that a bank will give you an umbrella when it's sunny, and take it away when it rains. The system was rotten to its core.

I didn't really want to start naming and shaming the bank manager in question. I haven't seen him for ages and I guess he was only doing his job. I'm sure he wasn't doing anything illegal, even though I felt it was unethical. But it did start me thinking. I've never been one just to sit around and grumble when I see something going wrong. If I come across a problem, my immediate reaction is to work out a way to solve it. But what could I, a small businessman from Burnley in Lancashire, do to tame the massive beast that was the worldwide financial system? It was a David and Goliath situation. Or maybe that should be Dave and Goliath. Whatever: in situations like that, Goliath usually wins.

And yet the idea wouldn't go away. There were instances of Goliath coming a cropper, weren't there? I thought of my hero Richard Branson taking on British Airways. Clearly I couldn't really make the banks start going about their business differently; clearly I couldn't take on a financial system that spanned the entire globe and in which the most powerful people in the world had vested interests. But perhaps I could prove to people that there might be a better way to go about things. Perhaps I could show that the status quo could be challenged. The bankers were over £50 billion in debt. The systems they were using had been shown to be flawed. If, in a small way, I could suggest a different way to do things, and show that it worked, perhaps other entrepreneurs across the country could do the same. The Establishment would have to take notice. They'd *want* to take notice. Wouldn't they?

The seed of an idea had been planted. I would set up a small bank in the centre of Burnley. I would apply everything I'd learned during my twenty years in business. I would offer a better rate of interest than any other high street bank. I would lend to local businesses who were struggling to get credit from their regular banks, and whose livelihoods were on the line. I wouldn't lend money that I didn't have. The big banks try to instil confidence in their customers by setting up shop in impressive buildings that make people think they're safe and secure. My tiny bank couldn't do that, so I had to instil confidence some other way. I would personally guarantee every last penny that my customers deposited with me. If I lost the money, the jeopardy was mine, not theirs. As far as I can tell, that's how it *should* be. And although this was, in part, a way of helping the local community, it would still be a business. The whole thing would be a failure if it lost money at the end of the day, and if that happened, I'd take my hat off to the banks, admit that I could do no better than them and get back in my box.

But something told me that *wouldn't* happen. Something told me my idea was a good one. Mine would be the most liquid, best-funded bank in the world because we wouldn't lend what we hadn't got. I believed in it, and like I've already said, believing in yourself is half the battle. I knew plenty of people would think I was daft even to consider what I was considering. After all, what did I, Dave Fishwick from Burnley, know about the complex world of banking? Well, not much, I'll grant you. Perhaps I was breaking one of my golden rules. Perhaps I was entering a business without knowing it inside out. Perhaps the reputation I'd worked so hard for so long to build up would be gone in a matter of months. I knew that reputation takes a lifetime to earn and seconds to lose. For me, that was a much bigger deal than merely losing money.

Or perhaps, I really *could* make a go of it.

I decided that any profit my bank made at the end of 180 days – which was the longest I could reasonably stay away from my other businesses – would go to charity, instead of being dished out as big bonuses. And although I didn't really know how much profit such a venture would eventually achieve, I was sure of one thing: even if I only made £1 after all the overheads were paid, I'd be fifty billion and one pounds better off than the rest of the banks. (Not bad, eh?)

Mine would be a tiny, tiny bank. There was no way I could be bigger than the big boys. But perhaps that was an advantage. I was reminded of a theory of business that I was once told. It's called the Third Milk Round Theory, and I happen to know it's true because I know somebody who once did it. This acquaintance of mine got himself a milk round and everything went just fine. He'd get up of a morning, do his milk round, make money and he was happy as Larry. After a while, though, he began thinking to himself, like most people eventually do, 'How can I make a bit *more* money?' The answer seemed obvious: he'd take on a second milk round. So that's what he did. He got someone to work for him, got a second van, a second lot of milk... you get the picture. So he got the income from a second milk round, but out of that he had to start paying wages, and running the second vehicle, and when his employee went on holiday he had to pay someone to cover for him. All this gave him a fair bit of grief, but while he wasn't making twice as much money, he *was* making more money than when he just had the one milk round.

And so he decided to get himself a *third* milk round.

Now he had even more staff, more vehicles, more milk, more headaches. And because of all this, he found that the third milk round wasn't making him any more money than he was earning from his original round plus a little bit of the second. The Third Milk Round Theory shows us how easy it is for a business to get *too* big, and it's very important for a businessman to bear it in mind. If you're in business, you need to be sure that each time you increase in size, it's going to increase your profit. Like I've said: any fool can increase their turnover, but it's the bit in the middle that you need to be mindful of.

It seemed to me that there was another reason why a tiny, tiny bank was more desirable than a great big one. One of the great problems during the banking crisis was that the huge financial institutions that had got themselves into such a mess were simply too big to fail. They had so much public money tied up in them that if they were allowed to go under the consequences for the country would have been unthinkable. The last thing I wanted was for my bank to be too big to fail. If I got myself into a mess, I'd take it on the chin and sort it out from my own pocket. It was very important, therefore, that I kept it scaled down to what I could adequately manage if I was going to be responsible with the money that the people of Burnley could ill afford to lose.

So I couldn't be bigger than the other banks. But I *could* be better. The more I thought about it, the more it seemed like a good idea. I had money at my disposal. I wouldn't say that it was burning a hole in my pocket, but I would say this: using it to make a difference to my local community felt much better than building up a collection of Ferraris. I could no doubt spend my time trying to add another couple of zeroes to my bank balance, but what difference would that make to me? What could I do with more wealth that I couldn't do now? When I thought about it like that, the decision almost made itself.

If you really want to bore me – to make my eyes glaze over and have me politely suppressing a yawn – give me a business plan. People are always being told to write these bloody things, and seem to think that the longer and more detailed they are, the better. Bollocks. If you really have to write a business plan, make sure you can put it down in two paragraphs. If you can't, it's probably a rubbish idea. Come to think of it, two paragraphs is probably a bit too wordy. If I had to write a business plan for my main business it would be four words long, 'Sell lots of minibuses'. So ignore anyone who tells you your business plan needs 'vision statements' and 'economic assessments' (whatever they are). You and I both know that your 'estimated turnover' is just a wild stab in the dark, so why don't we just dispense with the bullshit and get down to brass tacks. Scribble your 'business plan' out at the kitchen table on the back of an envelope, or, even better, the back of a bill. That way you get something out of the paper, and it shouldn't take more than about a minute.

That's what I did. A tiny plan for a tiny bank. It read like this:

1. Pay ordinary people more interest than they can get anywhere else.
2. Guarantee every pound they put in with a pound of my own money.
3. Lend money to local businesses, like Big Roy's, that can't get credit anywhere else.
4. Get it into profit in 180 days and give what we make to charity.

If I could prove that it could be done on a tiny scale, maybe it would encourage other like-minded businessmen to have a go themselves, and loosen the stranglehold the banks have on us all. I'd ignore the fact that I knew nothing about banking. I'd find a way around the obstacles that I knew would be put in my way. As long as I believed in myself, and I approached the whole thing with a nice big bucketful of common sense, what could possibly go wrong?

LICENCE TO FILL

(Your Boots)

I'd like to tell you about Betty. Her story is one that, for me, goes right to the heart of everything that is wrong with the big banks, as well as everything that I hoped to achieve with my tiny one.

Betty is an elegant, dignified widow, but not rich. She's a Burnley girl through and through, who volunteers at the local hospice and seems to me to represent everything that is good about the local community. In 2000, not long before her husband died, Betty invested her retirement nest egg with one of the big banks. Now, don't get me wrong: Betty's no fool. But by her own admission she has no understanding of stocks and shares. Why should she? It's not her game. She and her husband told the bank in question that they wanted this money to be invested in something safe and secure. It was all they had, after all; and they were clearly not high-risk investors wanting to gamble the savings that were intended to see them out.

Despite all this, Betty and her husband's nest egg was invested in stocks and shares that fluctuated wildly. And in the wrong direction. Her husband sadly passed away; the investments that were supposed to be safe and conservative plummeted. A massive chunk was wiped off the value of Betty's money; when she cashed in her investment, she was substantially poorer. You don't need me to tell you that for a retired widow, this is a terrible situation to be in.

But here's the thing. The commission that she paid to the bank for the honour of taking out the investment that lost nearly half her money is still swilling around in the bank's coffers – or, more likely, has been paid out as part of a bonus to the 'experts' who advised her so badly in the first place. It seems to me that Betty had paid for the pleasure of losing her money, whereas the people who'd *got* paid for it, and should therefore have shouldered the risk, got away scot-free. If that's fair, I'm a Chinaman.

I wanted to set up a bank that someone like Betty could trust. A good bank. A bank with a conscience. Not a charity – not by any means – but a tiny little financial institution that takes its responsibilities seriously and treats its customers, and their money, with respect. Was I being impossibly naive in imagining that such a thing could actually work? I've no doubt plenty of people thought I was. If it was a good idea, surely someone else would have done it? And if they hadn't, surely that proved that bankers have always been the grasping baddies we know and love?

Well, no, actually.

It's difficult to pinpoint which was the first savings bank, or when the concept came into existence. All the very early banks, however, had one thing in common: they were intended only for the rich, and not for the ordinary working man and woman. The tiny sums that the struggling members of the working class might be able to deposit were of little interest to the great merchants of the day. In 1810 all that changed, thanks to a Scottish church minister called Dr Henry Duncan.

I'm no church minister, but I can't help feeling a good deal of affection for Dr Duncan. He was ordained as minister in the Scottish parish of Ruthwell at a time of great austerity. Great Britain had spent huge amounts of money fighting the French; rural communities were struggling on account of the Industrial Revolution; in order to remain competitive, farmers knew they had to invest in the new machinery of their trade, but it was expensive and times were hard. The country was crippled by war expenditure and tiny businesses were struggling. Ring any bells? Duncan's parishioners were grindingly poor. There wasn't much work around, and it wasn't well paid. Top whack for a day's labour was about 5 pence in today's money, and the price of food was rocketing, not least because harvests had been bad for several years. There are no good times to be poor; but if there were, this wouldn't have been one of them.

Henry Duncan didn't like the idea of handouts. He understood that they were nothing more than sticking plasters. They didn't treat the root cause of the problem. It would be much better, he decided, if he could help his parishioners help themselves. Give them a chance to regain some of their dignity. What if they could save small sums in a community bank, and be paid the same rate of interest as anyone else? What if their money could be put to good use in the community, helping businesses grow and thereby improving the lot of everyone, not just the business-owners? Surely that would both encourage thrift and be a genuine force for good...

Dr Henry Duncan's tiny community bank was a massive success. In its first year, it received just over £150 in deposits, which is remarkable given the daily wage at the time. He called it the Trustee Savings Bank – the TSB – and within five years the model had been adopted in different communities all over the country. As the TSB evolved, its deposits were invested in increasingly safe securities, as opposed to the larger commercial banks who could be somewhat more profligate and riskier with their investments. The TSB remained this way until the 1970s. I don't know about you, but I find it sad that a bank which started out with such good intentions was then merged with a big commercial bank like Lloyds.

So, my idea of community banking wasn't a new one. It had worked before; and although the world had changed massively since Henry Duncan's day, I was convinced that it could work again. That thought gave me a bit more confidence as I started taking my first steps into the murky world of banking.

There are people who might try to tell you that setting up a business when the worldwide economy is flatlining and the country is teetering in and out of recession is a foolhardy endeavour. I don't see it that way. In my mind, setting up a business is like buying a farm. If you decided you wanted to be a farmer, and went out to buy yourself a hundred acres of farmland, chances are you'd be doing it as a long-term project, not something you'd mess around at for a couple of years before moving on to something else. You'd most likely intend to be at it for thirty or thirty-five years. Now, in that time, you might reasonably expect to have a few bad years. The crops might fail; your cows might drop dead; you might have a dry season or two. Does that mean your farming business has been a failure? Of course not. Would it put you off buying the farm? No.

The same is true of any business. I can understand why people are disinclined to start up new ventures when the economy is faltering, but it's important to remember that you are going to be doing whatever you're doing – whether it's milking cows, building buses or selling flowers – for a good few years to come. You mustn't worry too much about having a few bad years here and there. If your idea's good, and your business is well run, you'll come out the other side without too much trouble. And if you can make it work in difficult times, you'll make a fortune when things turn round – which they will, I promise.

So, the idea of starting up a new venture when the economic climate was, to put it mildly, difficult, didn't worry me too much. In fact, from a certain perspective, it was the main reason I was doing it in the first place. But I had to be honest with myself. The truth was that although I loved the idea of setting up my own bank, I really had no clue how to go about it. Where should I start? Who should I approach? What should I do first? I had no experience in banking. No qualifications. I knew the businesses I was in like the back of my hand; but the world I wanted to break into already felt like a closed shop. It was possible, I supposed, to hire lots of expensive consultants and advisers; I had no doubt that I could spend tens of thousands of pounds in the course of a few phone calls and not even move away from square one. I didn't much fancy that. So I did what everyone does when they want to find out about something. I Googled it.

'How to open a bank'. You should type it in yourself and see what comes up. Plenty of suggestions and adverts for how to open a bank *account*, of course, which is hardly surprising. Those chaps on the high street really want your business, remember. There were some tempting opportunities to open a *Swiss* bank account (not much need for them in Burnley and Nelson). Number two on the list told me how to *rob* a bank. Tempting – the banks had robbed us, after all – but I didn't much fancy an all-expenses-paid trip to Strangeways. The only entry that appeared on the screen that was in any way relevant to what I was looking for was for an American firm called Banking 4 Bankers. Not Banking 4 Joe Bloggs; Banking for *Bankers*. Closed shop? I think you could say that.

Surely, I thought to myself, I couldn't be the only person to have had this idea. Surely *someone* must have set up their own bank in recent years and might be on hand to give me a bit of advice on how to go about it. I dug a little deeper and discovered that the piece of paper needed by anybody wanting to set up a bank of their own was called a banking licence, issued by the Financial Services Authority, or FSA. The FSA is an independent body set up to regulate financial institutions in the UK. Its stated objectives are: market confidence, financial stability, consumer protection and reduction of financial crime. Well, two out of four ain't bad. If I wanted to set up a bank that intended to take deposits from local people, I would need the FSA to issue me with a banking licence.

And that, surely, wouldn't be too hard, would it? I sent off for the application form.

I'll level with you. Paperwork's not my thing. Never has been. When I see a pile of forms and documentation, my instant reaction is to assume that someone's surrounded a small nugget of something interesting or useful with a great big bucket of bullshit. Can't be doing with it. Always have been that way, always will be.

The FSA's application form for a UK banking licence is thousands of pages long and rises about two feet high off the table. It's a monster. Take one look at it and, if you're anything like me, you'll start to wonder if it's specifically designed to put people off even beginning to fill in the bloody thing in the first place. I can't help thinking that 99.9% of people would take one look at it, say 'Sod that for a game of soldiers', and give up on their grand plans to start a bank. Maybe that has something to do with the fact that, in the past hundred years, only a single banking licence has been approved in the UK. This was in March 2010, to a new operation called Metro Bank. Metro Bank is not a community bank like mine, but, significantly, its whole business model centres around a perception that customers are fed up to the back teeth with the old kind of banking and are looking for something different. I found that encouraging in itself, as it meant I was on the right track with my own ideas. The business was co-founded by Vernon W. Hill II, who started Commerce Bank in the United States and built it up from a single office in Philadelphia in 1973, to 500 offices and assets of $50 billion. Commerce Bank prides itself on customer service, and has won any number of consumer awards. His aim has been to bring a similar business model to the UK. Metro Bank's focus is on customer service and convenience; they refer to their outlets not as branches, but as stores; and their aim is to reintroduce the more traditional banking model and to encourage deposit-based lending.

There are plenty of differences, of course, between Vernon W. Hill II's venture and David Fishwick's, not least that the executive team of Metro Bank is filled with high-flying bankers with whole careers' worth of banking experience. I couldn't tell you what it had cost them to get their banking licence, or how much capital they had to raise in order to start up their business, but I do know that it would have been many, many times more than the sum my tiny community bank would have to play with. They weren't initially setting up in depressed parts of the country, but in London. What's more, their saving and borrowing rates were not spectacularly different from those of the established banks. Their ethos might have been similar to mine, but in other ways they were from a different world.

Anyhow, the UK banking licence application form is nothing if not off-putting. So off-putting that the usual way of acquiring a banking licence is to buy up a company that has one among its assets. Perhaps I should have realised that if people find it more straightforward to do *that*, my hopes of getting a banking licence in the bag within a few weeks was a tiny bit optimistic.

Sometimes in business you have to find a way round the obstacles that other people put in your way. Other times, you just have to cross them. It was perfectly obvious that the FSA wouldn't even consider me for a banking licence if I failed to dot the *i*s and cross the *t*s of every single one of their thousands of pages.

I approached a firm of solicitors – Keith Arrowsmith and Chris Moss of JMW – high fliers whose offices are housed in a Manchester skyscraper. I had spoken to them about the bank I wanted to create, and they had immediately got it. They offered to help me with my banking application for next to nothing because of my intention to give the profits to charity at the end of the 180 days. If the Bank of Dave was to become profitable, that was the sort of support I truly needed. They carefully filled in every last page of that application form, and we sent it back to the FSA.

We ran into our first stumbling block on page 2.

One of the first questions they ask is: how much money will your bank have in reserve. If you've read the previous chapter, you'll understand what they're asking: how much hard cash will we have in the bank to enable us to pay back our depositors should they want to withdraw their money. It's not an unreasonable question. If a bank is going to lend money out, there needs to be some way of ensuring they can refund their depositors at any point. We've already seen how a run on the bank can be a disaster for the whole economy and it's absolutely right that a bank should have sufficient liquidity to pay back its depositors. I wanted the Bank of Dave to be *better* than all the others. The last thing I wanted to do was to risk not being able to pay back anyone who entrusted me with their money. It's a point of principle. From day one, I've always said that I would rather cut off my right leg than have a single person lose a single pound having had faith in the Bank of Dave. And so, in response, our application made it clear exactly what we intended to do.

The Bank of Dave, I explained, would be 100% funded. What does that mean? Simply this: for every pound a depositor put into their account, I would personally back it up with a pound of my own money. None of this fractional reserve nonsense. No smoke. No mirrors. Every deposit matched, pound for pound.

Not good enough.

The minimum requirement, it transpired, was 10 million euros, to be placed in a separate account where it can't be touched.

100

But this was to be a tiny, tiny bank! I tried to explain that there would never, not in a month of Sundays, be 10 million euros of activity. A million, perhaps. Maybe a million and a half. And in any case it didn't matter. We were to be 100% funded. *A hundred per cent!*

I want you to think about that for a moment. Imagine a great big bank – one of the ones you see on the high street. How much of their customers' money do you reckon they have on deposit? Billions? You bet. Compared to that, 10 million euros is nothing. It seems to me to offer hardly any security. But for a small, community bank like mine, it's an impossible hurdle. To my eyes, this was another piece of evidence that the system was stacked massively in the favour of the already wealthy and the status quo, and I was determined to fight it. I wasn't going to give up on getting myself a full-blown banking licence, but I knew that if I wanted to get this thing off the ground, I was going to have to think outside the box. I'd probably step on a few Establishment toes in doing it, but fuck 'em – they'd soon get over that, wouldn't they?

Wrongly or rightly there are lots of people who, when they talk, I don't listen. I can count on one hand the people in this world whose opinion I truly trust and to whom I really, really pay attention. One of them is my wife, Nicky. If I want to discuss something with a properly intelligent individual, I turn to her.

She's very different to me in many ways. For a start, she's a qualified bio-medical scientist with a bagful of O-levels,

A-levels and diplomas. But it's her outlook I value more than anything else. Her view of the world. She's not distracted by flighty, unimportant things, and while she would never dream of telling me that I *couldn't* do something, she'd equally never shy away from giving it to me straight, exactly how she sees it. As the idea of the Bank of Dave started to evolve in my mind, I shared my thoughts with her, and was relieved to get a positive response in return.

I knew, however, I couldn't just go into this thing blind, even with Nicky's blessing. I certainly wouldn't do it in any other business. If I were setting up a pub from scratch, I'd go and get a job in a pub. I'd learn the ropes, teach myself about the products, find out what the customers want and where the best deals are coming from. I'd keep an eye on the competition and work out which bits of what they're doing were working, and which bits weren't. However, the chances of me walking on to the trading floor at RBS and cadging a couple of months' work were, to put it mildly, slim. If I was going to check out the competition, I'd have to do it some other way. And if you want to learn about banking in the UK, there's only one place to go. London.

It was early on in my quest to set up the Bank of Dave that I heard about an outfit called Zopa. This was a relatively new financial institution based in London and created by the team who had set up the internet bank Egg. They wanted to do something new, different and interesting. The idea they came up with was not a bank, but very *like* a bank. I travelled down from Burnley to see them, and to find out a little more about what Zopa does.

I expected Zopa's offices to be rather splendid – an impressive, imposing facade with tinted windows and all the rest of it. I mean, that's what financial institutions are supposed to look like, aren't they? I couldn't have been more wrong: Zopa was little more than a big room filled with very busy people. Already I was warming to them. If *I* was paying a company to help invest my money, I don't think I'd really want them to be blowing their turnover on big fancy office blocks that they didn't need. I liked that there were perhaps only thirty people working for this great big operation, and I liked that they could call to each other across the office if they needed to, much like the guys and I do back at the garage; everything was frenzied and happening in real time, with none of the 'Go upstairs to the third floor, bang on the door and see if Mr Wotsit might have five minutes sometime this afternoon' rubbish that I'm sure goes on elsewhere. Already I could see that these guys were a bit more on my wavelength.

A friendly young man called Giles Andrews sat me down in the middle of this open-plan office. Like me, he used to be in the car business, and I think we hit it off OK. Giles talked me through their business model. Zopa, he explained, does almost all the things a bank does, without actually *being* a bank. From our vantage point in the middle of his office, he pointed out members of staff seated at different desks, all carrying out the different roles: underwriting, marketing and finance, IT, customer service. Giles explained that Zopa thinks of itself as a 'marketplace', matching savers with money to deposit with businesses who need to borrow money. Perhaps that doesn't immediately sound like what a bank does. But think about it. When you put your wages into a bank account, you don't just expect the bank to keep it safe, you expect it to pay you some interest. The bank does this by lending your money out. The difference between Zopa and a regular bank, it seemed to me, was one of pretence. A regular bank *pretends* that all your money is sitting in your account when it isn't really. Zopa is upfront about what it does. When you deposit your money with Zopa, you *know* that they're going to invest it in order to give you the return you want. You can't simply walk into its offices and then withdraw the money you've given it. It's not, to use the jargon, a 'deposit-taking institution'. It's a middle-man, acting as a link between savers and borrowers. And a bank, at its heart, is exactly that. It just pretends to be something else.

And because its overheads are smaller than a bank's, Zopa can pass this on to both the borrowers and the lenders. It charges a small fixed fee to borrowers – £118.50 at the time I visited – and it charges lenders 1% annually. Over the years it has had about 50,000 borrowers and 30,000 lenders, and has lent about £150 million. The individual loans have not been massive: the average amount borrowed and the average amount lent is the same figure of about £5,000. A small sum, but one that can make a real difference to a struggling business that can't get credit elsewhere. Zopa's job is not only to effect the introduction, but also to manage the risk that its lenders are taking – to vet potential borrowers on an individual, one-by-one basis. To make sure they are who they say they are and that they're likely to pay back what they say they're going to pay back. In short, to ensure that the loans are good. You would think, of course, that this is something *all* financial institutions which make their money from providing loans would do. Recent history tells us we'd be wrong to assume this. We've already seen how banks can slap AAA ratings on loans that, in the cold light of day, perhaps wouldn't achieve such a glowing report, especially if the ratings agency wasn't hungry for more of the bank's business in the future. And the proof of the pudding? The average rate of bad debt for the banks is around three times the average rate of bad debt Zopa experiences. It is showing that it is possible to lend money more responsibly than the banks have been doing; and that it's possible to pay savers a better rate than the banks seem able to offer.

Giles explained to me about a bank's 'spread'. This is the difference between the rate at which they lend money out and the interest they pay their savers. It's their bit in the middle. At the time of writing, the banks' spread is around 10%: they lend money out at around 12 or 13%, and they pay their savers 2 or 3%. Zopa's aim, if it is to remain competitive, is to make sure that its fees are less than that spread. You might think that's not terribly difficult, given that there is 10% to play with. You'd be right.

I suggested to Giles that for my bank to charge 7% and pay 5% would be entirely feasible. Take out 1% for your overheads and the 1% that's left is profit. He agreed, but with some reservations. Firstly, he said, it wasn't easy for a bank to keep its overheads down (I had a different opinion about that); secondly, I would have the issue of making sure money was there for my savers to withdraw if they wanted to (but I was going to match their deposits pound for pound out of my own money – something the banks would never do); and thirdly, I needed to factor into my calculations that some of my loans would turn bad, and there needed to be enough wriggle room for this.

At the time I visited Giles, I was in the middle of trying to get to grips with my banking licence application form, and I wondered how Zopa had fared with the FSA. To my surprise, Zopa wasn't even regulated by the authority, even though it wanted to be. As they weren't a proper bank, they hadn't needed to apply for a banking licence. Or, to put it in Giles's words, 'We didn't have to go through the same degree of pain as you're about to.'

Great.

Zopa may not have had to apply for a banking licence, but Giles knew people who had gone down that path and knew also that it was a very time-consuming business that most people delegated to professionals who cost an arm and both legs. I asked him for a ballpark figure. Millions of pounds, he told me. And a timescale? Two to three years. All this, just to be allowed to start a business. A lot of the banking licence application form, Giles observed, revolved around the business itself, and putting together a bloody business plan. I rather suspected that the FSA wouldn't share my 'back of the envelope' approach. It would want to know everything about my executive team. But at the moment, my executive team was me.

'So who's doing your credit risk assessment?'

Me.

'Fraud risk assessment?'

Er, me.

Maybe, Giles said, the FSA would engage with me seriously on the basis that they'd never seen anything like it before. I think he was just being polite.

Giles obviously knew what he was talking about, so I wondered if he thought there was a way round me having to jump through the FSA's hoops. His response wasn't very encouraging. 'I don't think so,' he said, 'if, ultimately, you're going to be taking deposits.' His take was that I needed to explore other ways of raising the money I wanted to lend out — maybe by bringing other shareholders into the business, or even by following a model similar to Zopa's. I wasn't keen. Businesses weren't alone in getting a raw deal from the banks. Savers were too, and half of my battle was trying to give the ordinary people of Nelson and Burnley a more generous rate of interest on their savings. I certainly wasn't setting out to make rich people richer.

As far as I could tell, the FSA banking licence existed to protect consumers. If a financial institution that has a banking licence loses any of its customers' money, the government will guarantee to pay that money back, up to a maximum of £85,000 per person. But my plan was to personally guarantee every last penny my customers deposited with me and therefore I didn't need to take advantage of this guarantee. Surely the FSA would take that on board?

Maybe, said Giles. More likely, the FSA's view would be that a bank is a bank and they all have to toe the line.

I could tell just by looking around me that Zopa was a tightly-run ship. I liked that. I liked the way money was clearly not being wasted. I was interested to know what Giles's thoughts were on the thorny issue of bankers' bonuses. He agreed that in times of economic hardship, nobody liked to see a small group of people being paid large amounts when everybody else was struggling. But he was also of the opinion that the bonuses themselves weren't the main issue, but rather were a symptom of a wider problem. That problem was something that I'd suspected for a long time: banks are very badly-run businesses. They are bloated and inefficient. Whereas a small business owner must, of necessity, keep his eye firmly on every last penny that's being spent, the banks don't do this because they don't have to. And why don't they have to? Because they know that if they run into difficulties, they'll be bailed out by the taxpayer.

My visit to Zopa was at once encouraging and dispiriting. I could see that it was clearly possible for other kinds of banking to exist, but despite Giles's supportive noises, I could tell that he thought the chances of my getting a banking licence – at least without spending millions and waiting years – were as tiny as the bank I wanted to set up. And *without* a banking licence I was, not to put too fine a point on it, shafted. I wouldn't be able to take deposits. Without deposits, I wasn't a bank.

I continued knocking on London doors. One of those doors belonged to Andrew Hilton, the joint founder of the Centre for the Study of Financial Innovation, a not-for-profit banking think tank. Let's just say that him and me were like chalk and cheese. I asked him the question that was at the front of my mind: what chance have I got of getting a banking licence?

'Absolutely none.'

He asked me where I was from.

'Burnley,' I told him.

What university had I gone to?

'Er… I didn't go to one.'

So I wanted to open a bank without having been to Oxford or Cambridge? I don't think he found the idea funny. I think he found it ridiculous. Because I came from Burnley, I wasn't clever enough.

I decided to enlighten Mr Hilton about how things are when you're not born with a silver spoon rammed up your arse. People from Burnley, I told him, don't normally get the chance to go to Oxford and Cambridge. Up there, you leave school, you start work the following day – if you're lucky. That's how it works – we don't, in the main, have the same opportunities as others. My little lesson in the way of the world fell on deaf ears. Clearly, I was told, if I hadn't been to Oxford or Cambridge, I wasn't clever enough to open a bank.

Qualifications. I had wondered how long it would be before

someone used my lack of them as a stick to beat me with. I was well prepared for it. I'm not knocking qualifications. For some people they mean the earth and I totally understand that. But when someone turns up for a job interview with me, CV in hand, the first thing I do with their carefully-worded document is put it to one side. I don't do that to be arrogant or ignorant; I do it because I'm much more interested in finding out face to face what they can bring to the party than reading a list of grades and achievements. A bucket of common sense is worth much more to me than a fancy degree.

This bloke explained that he'd got to his late twenties before he even left education. How old was I when I left school? Sixteen, I told him. I kept quiet about the fact that I'd made my first million by the time I was in my late twenties; and I held back from asking him how successful he thought that a City full of university educations had been in stopping the banks from making any mistakes. But I certainly wondered whether, even if I had left school at fifteen, I could do any worse than that bunch of idiots. If a few years at Oxford or Cambridge are what you need to fuck up quite so monumentally, thanks but no thanks.

'Are you an actor?' he asked me. I think he genuinely thought he was being scammed by Ali G, or at least that this was a more likely explanation for our conversation than some bloke with no letters after his name from Burnley wanting to set up a bank. I left in no doubt that he thought I was wasting my time and his. I suppose I could have been despondent, but I wasn't. As far as I was concerned, he didn't warrant listening to; he wanted sticking upside down in a wheelie bin and ignoring.

If Giles and his setup at Zopa represented the Young Turks of the banking industry, David Buik – whose door was the next I went knocking on – was head of the old guard. In the middle of the banking crisis, he was Sky News's analyst and I'd watched him on telly every day of the week. A market analyst with inter-dealer brokers BGC (no, I'm not sure what that means either), David had been in the City for half a century. He was, and I hope he won't mind me saying it, the archetypal ex-public-school City banker. Quite what he thought of Dave from Burnley turning up full of ideas to take him and his mates on at the banking game I couldn't rightly say. I'm pretty certain, though, that he had his doubts as to whether it could succeed.

That's not to say he didn't agree there was a problem. In the future, he told me, he saw it becoming increasingly difficult for banks to make the kind of small loans to small businesses that I wanted to make. They'd be able to lend great huge chunks of money to governments, but not to do the job that the average man in the street expects of them. I gave him my sales pitch: that I wanted to lend money to struggling local business, but also that I wanted to do it responsibly. This meant making proper, informed decisions about who I lent my bank's money to by looking them in the eye, visiting their premises, finding out if their loans would go towards something that was good value, and helping them out with a bit of advice if I could. David instantly recognised what

I wanted to do as being an old-fashioned style of banking. 'Many retired bank managers,' he said, 'will tell you that they never, ever lent to anybody they didn't know.' But it doesn't work like that any more, he explained, the reason being that banking is now a major global business that is done largely by ticking boxes and pressing keys on the computer. And if the computer says no, then tough.

It was this kind of banking, I realised, that the FSA and its banking licence was geared towards regulating. My small-scale, community bank was a different kettle of fish. David seemed to agree that there was a market for the sort of institution I wanted to set up, but he was quite adamant about one thing. On no account would I *ever* be able to call my bank a bank. Not without a banking licence, and my chances of getting one of those were looking smaller and smaller with each person I spoke to.

I left David's office with these words ringing in my ears, and also with an unnerving prediction he had made. I'd been wondering if he thought anything the banks or the FSA were doing in the wake of the financial crisis was likely to stop history repeating itself. 'I think,' he had told me, 'there will probably be fewer failures, at least for some time.'

But will it stop it completely?

'No, of course it won't. You're never going to stop the banking system from blowing up from time to time.'

A refreshingly honest take, I thought, from a true City insider. I don't know about you, but I can't decide what I find more terrifying: the fact that the bankers know how fragile their system is, or the fact that they just accept banking crises like the one that has just caused so many people so much misery as inevitable. Because the way I saw things, it didn't have to be inevitable at all.

The Hideaway is a jazz club tucked away in a quiet mews behind Streatham High Street. It's bohemian and hip: certainly not, at first glance, the kind of place you'd expect to find a stalwart of the banking industry. But in fact, it's not only frequented by a banker who would, finally, give me the thumbs up; it's owned by one. Roy Ruffler is the brains behind the Ruffler Bank, which has now been bought out by a London-based investment fund called AnaCap Financial Partners, but for forty years it was a small bank with a single branch in Surrey, offering decent rates to investors and specialising in lending to small businesses. I couldn't help noticing that there were similarities between us. He had left school with not much in the way of qualifications – just a handful of O-levels – and had gone into the business of coin-operated machines. You know the type of thing: fruit machines, jukeboxes, pool tables. When he sold his company in 1969, Roy found that he didn't really get on with the new owners, and left after six months. His next venture was a bank of sorts, taking deposits mostly from family and friends and lending the money out to people who wanted to finance the purchase of the coin machines he knew so much about manufacturing and selling. Sitting in the Hideaway with him – where I felt a good deal more comfortable than I had done in any of the stuffy bankers' offices that I'd found myself in so far during my trip to London – I asked him how he had gone about it, and how it was that he was able to call himself a bank.

When he started the business, Roy bought a company off the shelf called Lordsvale Finance, and for many years he saw no reason to change it. In the 1970s, however, there was a banking crisis not unlike the one we've recently experienced. Big banks were going bust and people were losing deposits. The government decided that this couldn't continue and, in 1979, started bringing in legislation to try to stop it happening again. The Bank of England – this was in the days before the FSA – turned round to Roy and told him that because of this legislation he was going to have to return all his deposits. Roy was understandably not very keen to do this as it would mean the end of his business. He explained that he didn't really *have* many deposits – just a few from family, friends and people to whom he had been personally recommended – and asked them if there was an alternative. The only alternative, they told him, was for Lordsvale Finance to become a bank.

Roy asked them what he had to do. Was there an application form? Any rules? Nope, they told him. No application form. No rules. All Roy had to do was write a letter to the Bank of England and he was off. I couldn't help wishing I had his luck.

As time went on, more banks fell by the wayside. Each time this happened, they tried to work out what had happened and why, and a new piece of regulation was added to the pile in order to protect against the particular reason why that particular bank had failed. That's how the rule book by which banks were expected to operate was built up over the next twenty years.

When I first started to explain to Roy what I wanted to do, I think it's fair to say that he saw it as a pretty tall order. The rules and regulation were too labyrinthine; the system just wasn't set up to encourage tiny outfits like the one I wanted to set up, but was designed for the big boys. In his opinion, a tiny, tiny bank would be one that started out with capital of about £20 million. And that was before we even got round the issue of how to take money from the public if we didn't have a banking licence. What I was doing, he told me, was almost an impossible task. My view of the banking world was too simplistic. And I absolutely would *not* be able to call it a bank.

I was beginning to get used to people telling me that. I was also getting used to ignoring it.

The more we talked, however, the more Roy seemed to come round. He had gone against the grain when he set up Ruffler Bank, and he could see that I was going against the grain too. It was the people who did that, he told me, who generally ended up with successful enterprises. I explained to him, when he suggested that a million pounds was not a lot of money, that where I'm from a million pounds is another planet. It might not be much to a lot of people in London, but in my neck of the woods, where the average working man earns between £10,000 and £12,000 a year, it's an unimaginable fortune. You can buy a house for ten grand;

a million quid will buy you a street full. Roy was reminded of a time when a customer borrowed £300,000 from him to buy a street of houses in Sheffield – not a million miles from Burnley – and gradually, when he took on board that I was prepared to guarantee every pound deposited in my bank with a pound of my own money, he agreed I might have a chance of succeeding. The Ruffler Bank had a habit of requesting a personal guarantee of everyone who borrowed money from them; me giving a personal guarantee to depositors was very much in the same vein. And they wouldn't have dreamed of giving a loan based on a glance at a computer screen, but would visit every single person they lent money to in order to satisfy themselves that they were good for it, just as I intended to do.

In many ways, Ruffler Bank was the Bank of Dave of the 1970s. I left the Hideaway jazz club with Roy's good wishes ringing in my head, and an offer of advice any time I needed it. It meant a lot to me, because it was a small ray of optimism among all the clouds of pessimism that had gathered during my time in London. Roy hadn't said it would be easy; he hadn't said I'd definitely succeed. But he wanted me to, and he thought it could be done.

I had to bear in mind, however, that there were plenty of hurdles still to come. To get a banking licence would cost millions and take years. Without one, I'd be breaking the law if I accepted deposits from the ordinary folk of Burnley. And there was no way – *no way at all* – that I could call my bank a bank.

But these were problems for another day. I was trying to go back to the old-fashioned, bowler-hat style of banking. So what I needed was a bowler hat. I went to Savile Row to be fitted for a suit. And then I caught the train back to Burnley, more determined than ever before to prove the naysayers wrong, and get my tiny, tiny bank off the ground.

HOW TO BUILD A BANK

In the eastern part of central London, just north of the Thames and right in the heart of the Square Mile, sits the Old Lady of Threadneedle Street. This isn't a real old lady, of course: it's the Bank of England, the central reserve bank of the United Kingdom and the institution which, among many other things, issues bank notes and sets interest rates. It's a very impressive building.

The Bank of England has been situated in Threadneedle Street since 1734. It's thought to have been the first purpose-built bank in the world. It was built with security in mind. There are no adjoining buildings, and no windows on the ground floor. Up until 1973, troops of soldiers wearing bearskins would march into the bank every evening: a visible sign that this was a kind of fortress, a safe place for everything held within its vaults. It looks imposing. Strong. Secure.

You can understand why bankers would want to house their banks in buildings like this, and have traditionally done so. Think back to earlier in the book when we met Barry the Banker. His original plan was to look after people's gold for them. Now, if *you* had a pile of gold and you were going to entrust it to somebody for safekeeping, you'd probably want to know that it was somewhere thieves and vagabonds couldn't get at it. (We'll ignore, for the moment, the possibility that you've entrusted it to thieves and vagabonds in the first place.)

These days, of course, we don't deposit huge quantities of gold in our banks. We don't even deposit much cash. Our modern-day bank balances are just numbers on a computer. So why would banks want to house themselves in big, impressive buildings? What's the reason for doing so if they don't need to persuade you that men in stripy tops carrying swag bags aren't going to break in and steal all your hard-earned?

The answer is that it's not about you. It's about them.

We've seen how easy it is for our banks to fail. We've seen that they're like a house of cards: impressive when you look at it, but at heart extremely fragile and easy to collapse. But be honest. Before the banking crisis, is that really the image you had of them? Did they seem like precarious businesses that could be subject, like any other, to the vagaries of the world at large? Did it ever *really* seem possible that the banks could go bankrupt?

I'd suggest not. And part of the reason for that is the banks' well-practised and time-honoured ability to make themselves appear to be permanent, immutable institutions. They do this in lots of ways. They make themselves look serious and austere – clever men and women in business suits who have our best interests at heart. They remind us how long they've been in business, and what a rich tradition they have of solid, dependable financial security. A large part of this is achieved by the buildings in which they house themselves. You could travel the world and see any number of enormous banking buildings with classical columns and marble facades. It would be a bloody boring holiday, but there would be plenty of these buildings to look at. Making themselves look like they've always been there – and crucially that they always *will* be there – is one of the traditional banks' oldest marketing tricks. They want you to believe they're more solid than they actually are so that's what they make themselves look like. It's a very effective bit of spin.

But spin, of course, is what it is. It's no different from a car manufacturer showing you an advert with one of their vehicles speeding up a mountain track, or someone trying to flog face cream with pictures of models who aren't at risk of having a wrinkle for a good couple of decades.

Banking architecture has moved on. We still have some banks located in big stone edifices which look like they've been there for hundreds of years. Maybe nothing as impressive as the Old Lady of Threadneedle Street, but they certainly don't look like pound shops that might close down after a bad day's trading. If you were to pay a visit to Canary Wharf and have a look at some of the modern buildings where many of the banks have their headquarters (another boring holiday idea), you'd soon get the picture. These huge glass and steel towers, the modern equivalent of those marble-clad temples to money, are genuinely breathtaking. They are big, important buildings for big, important banks. Surely, nobody with the resources to set up shop somewhere like that could be anything other than trustworthy, solvent and liquid. Could they? I couldn't even guess what it costs to have space in one of these buildings, but I feel pretty confident it's an eye-watering sum of money. I remembered Roy Ruffler's observation that one of my biggest issues was going to be keeping my overheads down. Not squandering dosh on setting up in a skyscraper was, I felt, a good way to start.

Of course, you don't wander down to Canary Wharf every time you want to take a tenner out of the hole in the wall or speak to someone face to face about your banking affairs. For that we have the more familiar sight of the high street branch. Now, you'd be right to say that these branches don't, generally, display mighty columns and stately permanence. They don't house themselves in enormous skyscrapers of glass and steel. Have the bankers lost their taste for spin? Don't you believe it. In the course of setting up the Bank of Dave, I spoke to a regional manager from one of the big-name banks who informed me that the average cost of refitting a high street branch was, wait for it, £1 million.

Let's have a think about what that means. The average working man's wage in Burnley is between £10,000 and £12,000. So to refit a single branch takes something of the order of *a hundred years' worth* of one man's yearly wage. Now imagine that you were setting up a business. You want it to be a tightly run ship. You don't want to spend a single penny when it's not worth it. You wouldn't be doing anyone any favours by being profligate with your money. First things first, however. You need premises. Perhaps you need to do somewhere up. How much are you planning to spend on it? A million quid? Thought not.

If it was an ordinary company spending this sort of money, perhaps it wouldn't be so bad. If they want to waste their cash, more fool them. But it seems to me that the same thing doesn't hold for banks. They're not ordinary businesses, because as well as being money-making machines, they are guardians of our hard-earned wages. They have a responsibility to be careful with the money they have. When they spend a million quid doing up one of their branches, that's a million quid of your money. And when you look at your bank balance, and you wonder about the paltry rate of interest your bank has decided to pay you, you need to consider whether there might be scope for a bit more generosity, if they hadn't been so wasteful elsewhere.

The Bank of Dave, if it was to be successful, simply couldn't afford that sort of extravagance even if I'd wanted to indulge in it. It's in my DNA to find the best deal I possibly can for every bit of every business venture I turn my hand to. This venture, though, was different. It wasn't my money I was risking. It was – assuming I got round the thorny issue of being able to take deposits from local people in my community – the money of regular, hard-working folk who could ill afford for it to be spent on big old buildings and fancy soft furnishings. And every pound I spent on doing up my bank was a pound that I couldn't lend out to the local businesses that were so desperate for the money, and was a pound out of any money I might end up giving to charity at the end of my 180 days. Mine was a tiny, tiny bank, so I needed a tiny, tiny premises. Most importantly, I wanted to pay a tiny, tiny rent for it.

Property in Burnley isn't like property in London. As there's less money knocking around up here, prices are correspondingly lower. I felt confident that I'd be able to find premises at a price I liked, but they couldn't be any old where. I wanted to be in the heart of things. There was no point setting up a bank where nobody could see it or where people wouldn't talk about it. I wouldn't have the funds to advertise my presence – no TV spots with black stallions galloping dramatically across the beach for the Bank of Dave – so it was important to me that the bank should be visible to as many people as possible, and that it could rely on a certain amount of passing trade.

The first site I looked at was right next to a branch of a well-known high street bank. I liked the idea of being cheek by jowl with the enemy. It seemed appropriate, somehow. And who knows, we might be able to do each other a favour. You know the kind of thing – we could nip round and borrow a cup of sugar if we've run out and fancy a brew, and they could nip round and borrow some money, seeing as how they've got none left. It was a lovely building – double-fronted, and with a basement that actually stretched underneath the bank next door. Plenty of space, plenty of exposure. The only trouble was that it cost plenty of money. The rent and the rates would, all told, end up being a couple of grand a month.

While that might be peanuts to the big boys, for me it was a fortune. My eyes, to quote the old saying, had been bigger than my belly. It was too expensive. Thanks but no thanks. I had to set my sights a bit lower.

I looked at lots of much smaller places, mostly down side streets and above shops. They were very good value for money, and some of them even had safes already fitted which would save me a whole lot of work. They all felt a bit too out of the way, though – I needed passing trade if I was going to make a success of this – and with hindsight I realised that the safes would have been no good anyway: I would require a certain *type* of safe if I was to have any chance whatsoever of receiving the licences, documents and bits of paper necessary to build a bank. So while these places were cheaper, they weren't actually going to do the job.

The premises I eventually chose had none of these problems. Number 30, Keirby Walk is in the heart of Burnley, surrounded by everything that makes this town what it is. There are cafes and dry cleaners; Big Roy the jeweller has his shop a few doors down. Stroll up and down Keirby Walk and you'll find the people of Burnley going about their daily business. It's not flash; it's not genteel; it's a bit rough around the edges and no doubt there are plenty of people who would look down their noses at it. Which meant that for me, the location was perfect. I wanted to be in the thick of it. I wanted to be among the people I was helping, not a hundred metres up some skyscraper, pretending to be all-important while the money I should be lending out was being leached on expensive rent.

My own little marketing plan, such as it was, was to present myself as being *of* the people, not aloof from the people. One of us, not one of them.

Furthermore, the price was right. At least, it was after a bit of negotiation. I agreed a weekly price of £100 in rent and £30 in rates. Less than six hundred quid a month, and that included a basement – maybe I should call it a vault – where the Bank of Dave could stick its safe. Admittedly the basement wasn't *quite* high enough to stand up in, and the dirty old chicken shed out the back needed a bit of attention, but I reckoned we could live with that.

Number 30, Keirby Walk had formerly been a florist's shop. While the location and the price were just right, the interior wasn't. I needed to do a refit of my own, but I certainly wasn't about to go down the million quid route, or even the hundred grand route – although I'm sure there are plenty of consultants and interior designers who would have been more than happy to help me try. But it seemed to me that I didn't need consultants or designers, just a bit of common sense. I sat down and worked out for myself what I would need to get set up. Not, I decided, very much.

I figured that the one thing every bank *had* to have was a safe. If people were going to deposit cash with the Bank of Dave, I couldn't just stick it in a drawer and hope for the best, or take it back home and shove it under the mattress. But the Bank of Dave's vaults weren't like the Bank of England's. I didn't think we'd need anything too extravagant.

I did a bit of research into local safe retailers, and found that there was a tiny safe dealership in nearby Barrowford – Barrowford Safe & Lock Services. I knew nothing about safes. In the car dealership world, nobody uses them. Back when I was buying and selling used cars, there was never a time when I didn't have a couple of grand in cash in my back pocket. I never knew when I would need to pay cash for a car – like I've said, money talks – so my money was no good stuck in a safe somewhere. And if I had more than a couple of grand in cash, I was doing something wrong, because that money should have been converted into something sitting on my forecourt ready to be sold. To this day I haven't got out of the habit of keeping a wad of cash in my pocket. But I couldn't walk around with all my depositors' hard-earned in my jeans, so I got myself down to Barrowford and started asking questions. I explained that I was starting up a tiny bank, and was given a crash course in the different varieties of safe on offer, and what I would need for my little venture. I learned that different types of safe offered different levels of insurance. Some were good for cash, some were good for valuables. They needed fastening to the floor with certain fixings – I was literally learning the nuts and bolts of my new trade. It struck me that there weren't many bankers out there who knew anything like as much about this as my new friend in the safe shop. And there's a good reason for that, of course: most bankers have nothing to do with cash or valuables, but just with lines of figures on computer screens. I was going back to basics, though. My tiny bank needed a decent safe in its tiny vault.

Barrowford's was only a small shop – space was at a premium and these safes were large. The owner, Matthew Blackburn, explained to me how difficult it was for him to store all his stock. His wasn't the kind of business where you sell a safe every day, or even every week. Looking after them all was a big issue for him.

I'm always on the lookout for a good deal; but when it came to the Bank of Dave my nose for a bargain was becoming doubly sensitive, and I could spot an opportunity here. There was one safe in particular, the biggest in the shop. It was exactly the kind of safe that a bank would have – heavy, sturdy and almost impossible to move – and it was taking up a lot of room in this small shop. So I made Matthew an offer. Why didn't he, I suggested, store his safe in my vault. I'd store cash in it, and if he got a customer that might want to buy it, they could always come down to the bank to have a look at it. And if he managed to sell it, no problem: all he had to do was come and pick it up and drop me another one off. I offered him a few quid each year for renting it, which meant he was getting something for it on top of the free storage; and the Bank of Dave was getting a £7,000 safe for virtually nothing.

In business, I've discovered, there are often ways of coming to agreements like this that don't involve paying out a load of money you can't necessarily afford. It's just a matter of putting yourself in the other guy's shoes; of working out what you've got that he wants. You and I both know that a big bank would never go about 'buying' a safe in this way, and I suppose I wouldn't really expect them to. The point is more that the big banks are very inefficiently run businesses, and that they could perhaps learn something from this way of doing things.

As part of the FSA's application form for a banking licence, I had to state how the Bank of Dave would store the financial information of its creditors and depositors, and how I proposed to back up all this information. I don't doubt that what they had in mind was a complicated – and expensive – computer system. Perhaps they imagined data centres and lines of terminals. They probably expected the Bank of Dave to outsource its IT to some technical whizz kids who would charge me a bloody fortune to keep all my customers' details safe.

I had a different idea. I reckoned we needed one laptop and a couple of notebooks from the local stationers. The plan was this. We would enter the customer details into the laptop as the savings and loans came in and out during the day. Overnight, we'd keep the laptop in the safe. To back it up, at the end of each day we would write down the day's transactions, once in each book. This method of backup has a big advantage over data centres and complicated IT structures. A book, you see, doesn't crash. It doesn't require maintenance, engineers or electricity. We'd keep one of the books in the safe with the laptop. One of the Bank of Dave's staff would take the second book home with them. It struck me as being much more secure than any other system we could devise, and it had the added advantage of costing a few hundred quid for the laptop, and about a fiver for the books. We would have to be improbably unlucky for our homespun backup system to fail, and even if one of the books did get lost or destroyed, the only skill anyone would need to make a copy of the other one was the ability to read and write, or perhaps use a photocopier. The banking licence application form didn't have a box to tick that said 'Notepad', so my friendly solicitors had to ring the FSA and explain what we planned to do. I daresay the FSA found it a bit Heath Robinson, but I couldn't really imagine what objection it would have to my strategy.

So I had my safe sorted, and also my IT and backup system. But the Bank of Dave still had an old chicken shed out the back, and the rest of the interior left a bit to be desired. It was nothing, though, that a spot of elbow grease and a bit of new carpet wouldn't sort out. Richard Slater, a friend of mine with a PR business, had his team design a logo to go outside, and Mark the Builder and Gary the Painter did me proud, offering their services for nothing and charging me only the materials they needed to do the job, they were so keen to help out and see it work. Mark Lomas from Lomas Office Furniture gave us furniture for nothing. It was heartening. These weren't rich bankers on million-pound bonuses; they were lads on wages giving their time and products for nowt, just because they believed in what we were doing. After a couple of weeks of building, plastering, wiring and painting, the old florist's shop was unrecognisable. Its tiny glass frontage looked in to a simple plain counter, behind which there was a black screen to divide the customer area from the little desk at the back that would be the engine room of my bank, and behind that the chicken shed had been turned into another usable room. A tiny flight of stairs – mind your head – took you down into the vault. Nothing like the vaults of the Old Lady of Threadneedle Street – you had to hunker down a bit because of the low ceiling – but that was no bad thing in my book. The whole thing was simple and unpretentious. No bells. No whistles. It was everything I'd imagined and intended the bank to be.

The final bill for refurbishing the Bank of Dave was under £9,000. That included everything, from computers to carpets to clocks, and including all the paperwork we'd had done. I'll admit, we did get some people to help out for nothing, it being a community venture rather than a hard-nosed business one. But even if I'd paid the going rate for everything, there's no way we'd have been in the same ballpark that regional manager had been alluding to. In fact, by their standards, we were £991,000 under budget. It's not like we were even thereabouts – it wouldn't surprise me to learn that one of their branches probably spends more on desks or fishtanks than my complete refurb.

And I'll say it again. If I want a big expensive desk in my office at work, where I conduct my main business, it's not a problem. I can have anything I want. The reason it's not a problem is that there hasn't been a single year when my business hasn't made money. I've never posted a loss, and what I chose to do with my profits is my own business. More to the point, if I *do* go out and buy myself a nice desk, I'm not using taxpayers' money to finance it. If you want to buy yourself a nice car, and you've got the money to do it, then that's fine. But if you're going cap in hand to the government for some taxpayers' hard-earned to bail you out, you shouldn't be spending that money on a new Porsche. And even if you're a bank and you *haven't* had a bailout, you need to remember that you have a duty to be thrifty and sensible with the money that your depositors have entrusted to your care. I think most people would agree that spending £1 million on a branch refurb is very far from being thrifty.

Even if it achieved nothing else, I felt that the Bank of Dave had already proved one thing. It's perfectly possible to set up a branch with the correct vault, the correct safe and the correct insurances for just a few thousand pounds. I fully accept that a bigger branch would have bigger overheads – more computers, more furniture. But it's not going to be £991,000 more, is it? Fifty grand more, perhaps. A hundred grand even. But it's not going to be a million quid. There's a mystique about banking, and it's perpetuated by the banks themselves. It's amazing, though, how little you need to set yourself up. If *we* could keep our costs down dramatically, why the hell couldn't the high street banks? Why must they spend our money creating this facade, this modern-day equivalent of the gold-plated, stone-fronted banks of old, when that money could so obviously be put to better use? How can they be spending such immense sums on their tinted-window shop fronts, when they haven't got any money in their safes?

So I had a bank. At least, I had the premises for a bank. Unfortunately, as I was beginning to find out, having somewhere to set up shop, and the wherewithal to do it, is the easy bit. There was still the small issue of the rules and regulations put in place by the Financial Services Authority; the tiny problem of a banking licence; the awkward stumbling block that if I called myself a bank and started taking deposits from the locals of Burnley and its surrounding areas, I'd be breaking the law and had a very real chance of ending up in prison. I had the advice of the people I'd talked to in London ringing in my ears. Giles at Zopa had warned me that trying to get a licence would be a painful experience; Andrew Hilton had told me that if I hadn't been to Oxford of Cambridge I didn't stand a chance; David Buik had been adamant that on no account would I *ever* be able to call my bank a bank; and Roy Ruffler, who had otherwise been very supportive, had told me that a licence would cost millions and take ages.

But I didn't have millions. I didn't have ages. I wanted to put the Bank of Dave into profit in 180 days and I had no intention of going to prison in the meantime. Maybe it's just me, however, but there is something strangely invigorating about the world and his wife telling you that what you want to do can't be done. I am, at heart, an entrepreneur, and I truly believe that it's the main job of an entrepreneur to turn a 'no' into a 'yes'. I've almost lost count of the times in my life when it has been up to me to do this. I'll give you just one example.

If you travel to Colne near Burnley, you'll see the site of my main business, David Fishwick Van and Minibus Sales. I bought that land when I was in my late twenties and it was the making of me. When you buy a piece of land, there's all manner of tedious paperwork that goes with it. As I've already mentioned, I hate paperwork. I usually refer to it as 'dog shit'. I can't be doing with details, because so often they get in the way of the bigger picture. When I bought this land I didn't read the boring paperwork in any detail. If I had, I'd have seen that the land had no official entrance; and having no official entrance invalidated it for any kind of planning permission. The only vehicle you could get on to the site of my proposed new premises was a helicopter, and I didn't have one of those back then.

So, I didn't know what the problem with this land was, but I *did* know that there *was* a problem because it was going for such a good price. It's in the nature of anyone with a bit of entrepreneurial flair, however, that we don't look too deeply into things. If you do that, you're bound to find problems. Our job isn't to look for problems, but to solve them if and when we find them. If something's a good idea, I'll just jump in with both feet. I knew I wouldn't have been able to buy the land I'd bought, with no planning permission and for the price I'd agreed, without there being some kind of catch. And the catch was that I couldn't even drive a vehicle on to this plot that I had earmarked for selling them. I needed to set about trying to find a solution.

I soon discovered that the council had been wanting to acquire the corner of the land I'd just bought from the previous owner in order to build a roundabout. He had been stubbornly holding out for a massive amount of money in the belief that the council *had* to have it and would eventually be forced to pay what he wanted. It didn't happen. More to the point, the stalemate between him and the council meant that they wouldn't give him permission for an entrance. But when I took over the land, I knew I had a bargaining tool. I decided on a plan: I'd suggest to the council that I simply *give* them the small piece of the land they needed for a roundabout if they would *give* me the entrance and planning permission. It wasn't unlike the deal I'd struck on behalf of the Bank of Dave with regards to the safe. Something I wanted for something they wanted, without so much as a pound changing hands.

It was by no means a done deal. Even if the town council agreed to my suggestion, the parish council still had to approve the planning. I remember one of the town planners parking his old Honda Civic in front of my crappy little portable office at my garage in Nelson and coming inside to talk to me. I had a picture behind my swivel chair of the garage I was going to build and about which I was so excited. He sat down opposite me, looked at the picture, and said, 'Well, son, if I was you I wouldn't have taken the risk. You'll not get planning there. I'd pull out now.'

I felt deflated, like I was a balloon and someone had just let the air out. But then I spun round, looked at the picture behind my desk and then looked out of the little office window at the council man's £300, pile of shit, beaten-up 1970s Honda Civic. What was I going to do – give up just because this fella, a man who clearly had never taken a risk in his life, had told me it couldn't be done? No way. I was going to do what I had to do: turn a no into a yes.

I started courting the parish council, which was in charge of planning permission, and explained that my intention was to employ local people and manufacture a product – minibuses – that would help schools and hospitals and businesses, presenting all the positives of what I wanted to do so they couldn't say no. I made friends with the parish councillors. I drank tea with them, and ate endless slices of cake. And drank more tea, and ate more cake while they sat there doing their knitting. And all the while I was trying to persuade them that they'd be doing the area a great deal of good if they let me build my minibuses on this land; and tried to forget what Mr Honda Civic had told me in my office.

It worked. When the day came for my planning hearing, I walked into the room and the old dear who was head of the planning council smiled and waved at me. I knew then and there that it was in the bag, and I'd proved to myself that if *I* believed in something, I could safely ignore all the prophets of doom and the naysayers who were lining up to tell me it couldn't be done. When it came to setting up my little bank, nothing I'd learned would be of greater use than this. Believe in yourself, because if you don't, the job's over before it's even started. And don't listen to the people who say it can't be done. There's always, *always* a way. It's your job to find it.

Everyone was telling me that the Bank of Dave couldn't be called a bank. *Everyone* was telling me that I couldn't take deposits from ordinary people. *Everyone* was telling me that if I broke the rules, the powers that be would come down on me like a ton of bricks.

But I had no intention of breaking any rules. I just wanted to sidestep them. I wanted to do what I did best, and what I'd done throughout my whole business career. I wanted to turn a 'no' – the most resounding 'no' I'd ever received – into a 'yes'.

IF YOU CAN'T WIN... CHEAT!

At home, I have a small wooden bench. I call it my thinking chair. Everyone needs a thinking chair – a place nobody else comes to sit. My thinking chair is nothing fancy – the type of thing you'll see in any park – but the view it affords over the Lancashire countryside is very special. You can see fields and forests and just lose yourself in the peace and tranquillity.

Whenever I have a problem, it's here that I go to sit. I turn things over in my mind. I approach them from different angles. I try to work out a way of skirting round obstacles that, when you're surrounded by the hurly-burly of the working day, might otherwise seem insurmountable. It's here, sitting on this bench, that I'm able to remind myself that no matter what anybody tells you, no matter how surrounded you might be by pessimists and naysayers, there's *always* a way round any problem. It's just up to you to find it.

My problem was this: I wanted to set up a bank, but it was looking increasingly unlikely that I would get a banking licence in time, on budget, or even at all. Just because I had a building, and I'd decked it out with everything a bank needs, I didn't have an actual bank if I couldn't do what an actual bank does. I decided I needed to break the issue down into more manageable pieces. What was it, I asked myself, that a banking licence actually allowed me to do? What, when I got down to brass tacks, were the essential components of my – or indeed any – bank?

Firstly, I needed to be allowed to lend money. This was, after all, one of the main reasons I started the whole venture. But did I really need a banking licence just to lend money? The answer was no, and the reason I knew this was that I'd already been lending money for the last couple of years to those customers of mine who were finding it impossible to get finance from the banks to buy my minibuses, and whose plight had given me the idea of the Bank of Dave in the first place. I was able to do this by means of something called a Consumer Credit Licence. If David Fishwick Van and Minibus Sales was able to get one of these, then surely the Bank of Dave could too.

Secondly, I needed to be able to take deposits. The truth was that, if I really wanted to, I could have funded the bank myself by taking, say, a million quid of my own money and lending *that* out to the local businesses that needed finance. But really, this was against the ethos of what I wanted to achieve. Providing credit would, hopefully, just be one half of the bank's role in the community. I also wanted to let local people deposit their money with me and earn a much better rate of interest than they'd be able to get elsewhere on the high street, while playing their part in helping the local community. I wanted to prove that it was possible for a bank to be profitable without taking its customers for a ride. And because I wanted to do everything that a normal bank does, I wanted to be able to accept deposits from businesses too. But it was this thorny issue of taking deposits that would, I could tell, be my biggest problem. I can see the FSA's point – it does not want any old Johnny Come Lately popping up, pretending to be a bank, taking everyone's cash and then doing a runner. But equally, surely there was some mechanism that allowed genuine people to do this without having to pay the millions of pounds required to get a banking licence?

The third component of the banking licence was that it would allow me to take advantage of the Financial Services Compensation Scheme, the safeguard put in place by the government to insure up to £85,000 per person per institution against the banks losing their money. I didn't need to avail myself of the FSCS because I intended to guarantee every last penny of my investors' money out of my own pocket. I've already explained that in the world in which I have always operated, a handshake is as good as a contract. But I could hardly expect the people of Burnley, many of whom wouldn't know who I was and who could ill afford to lose their savings, to take my word for that. But perhaps if I could set up some kind of insurance policy, backed up by my own personal assets, that would offer my customers a cast-iron compensation scheme of their own, this would be a way round not having the FSCS compensation afforded by an official banking licence.

Lend money; take deposits from individuals; take deposits from other businesses; guarantee those deposits. I began to think of these four components as 'the Bolt': bolt them all together, and you can do everything a banking licence lets you do, without having the licence itself. Of course, I wasn't going to give up on my application to the FSA – I'm afraid I'm a bit too pig-headed for that – but I wasn't prepared to wait years or pay millions, not if there was a way I could sidestep the rules. One of my maxims has always been: if you can't win, cheat. The world and his wife was telling me that I couldn't be a bank if I didn't have a banking licence, that preserve of the stinking rich and the banking elite. I was determined to show that I could.

If that meant cheating, then so be it.

For the Bolt to work, I would have to address myself to each component separately. But first, there was a another hurdle to cross. This was as important to me as any of the others. Having been told by all and sundry that I absolutely couldn't call myself a bank if I didn't have a banking licence, I was completely determined that, by hook or by crook, I was going to have the word 'Bank' on the frontage of my little premises in Keirby Walk. Call it stubbornness – you probably wouldn't be far off – but it wasn't just vanity that made me so fixated on this. It was important that people realised I was a bank, and not some obscure financial institution that had nothing to do with ordinary members of the public. Without that four-letter word, the Bank of Dave was nothing.

There was not a single person who was prepared to agree with me that there *had* to be a way to put the word 'bank' on the front of the Bank of Dave. My own high-flying solicitors told me I'd be breaking the law if I did it; everyone I asked backed them up. But I simply couldn't believe there was no way round it. It's in my nature that when I'm presented with a supposedly unsolvable problem, it nags away at me, day and night, until I've found a way through it. So it was with that tiny four-letter word that was causing me such problems.

Bank.

It was, after all, only a word. How could it be illegal to use it? I was going to do everything a bank did, and I was going to be a damn sight more responsible about it than some of the institutions that could use the word with impunity. I talked it over with Nicky. Wasn't there, we thought to ourselves, a women's clothing store called Bank? Nobody was threatening to chuck *their* managing director into prison. Wasn't there a tube station called Bank? No one had cordoned it off with armed guards, or painted over its signs. OK, so I was taking the piss a bit. Obviously, the clothing store Bank wasn't a financial institution, and nor was Bank station. But there was a serious point. It seemed to me that the problem wasn't the word itself, but how it was used. And that got me thinking. I wasn't just asking people to bank with me, I was asking them to *trust* me, just as I would be trusting those to whom I lent money to pay me back. People wouldn't just be banking *with* me; they'd be banking *on* me.

So what if I had the words 'Bank *on* Dave' instead of the words 'Bank *of* Dave' emblazoned across number 30 Keirby Walk? Would I be up in front of the beak for that?

Armed with my new idea, I went to consult with an expert in intellectual property called Tony Catterall. There was, after all, no point in me trying to pretend I was an expert when I wasn't. Surround yourself with the best people, remember? Empower them to solve the problem. Tony's feedback convinced me I was on to something. I just needed a little something extra. I steeled myself, waiting to be told that I would have to get my hands on some other bloody bit of paper that would no doubt cost an arm and a leg. But no. What I needed was...a bit of punctuation. Not my strong point, to be honest, so he explained a bit more. First off, I needed some quotation marks,

"Bank on Dave"

Next, I needed an exclamation mark,

"Bank on Dave!"

If I wrote it like that, he told me, the phrase was clearly a slogan not a name. I could call my bank something boring, sensible and by-the-book – in the end I decided on Burnley Savings and Loans, hoping that we'd end up doing what it said on the tin – and emblazon my slogan across my premises in great big letters. Passers-by would be in no doubt as to who and what we were; and the powers that be couldn't touch us. I walked out of Tony's office grinning like the cat that got the cream – I really do love it when a plan comes together! Before long, I had the slogan "Bank on Dave!" printed in large white letters against a black background over the glass frontage of number 30 Keirby Walk, with the real name of my new bank, Burnley Savings and Loans, rather hidden away in the top right-hand corner of the glass. I had something else printed too, which I hoped would grab the attention of any passers-by. 'No other bank comes close, because we're not like any other bank! We're better!!'

Like I'd always thought: the Bank of Dave couldn't be bigger than Barclays, but it could be better. Trouble was that so far, it wasn't a bank at all. The Bolt was not yet in place.

Component number one was the Consumer Credit Licence. The CCL is issued by the Office of Fair Trading and it allows you to lend money. Every bank in the UK has one of these. Without it, nobody can lend. Different CCLs might include different categories – some, for example, are good for mortgage lending, others for personal loans. But without a CCL, nobody can lend money on a commercial basis. A Consumer Credit Licence isn't necessarily difficult to get – a tiny shop can get one if they want to offer simple credit services – but it's more difficult to get one that covers the kind of lending that the Bank of Dave was intending to perform. And it can be time-consuming. Having decided that I wanted to get the Bank of Dave into profit in 180 days, it was something approaching disaster when I consulted with my solicitors in the summer of 2011 to be told that it could take until Christmas to get the licence. I wanted to open for business in September.

It's always good to have a backup plan. Hang on, I thought to myself. Surely I already *have* a Consumer Credit Licence hanging on my wall at the minibus business. Couldn't I just use that?

Grave faces from the solicitors. That CCL was in the name of David Fishwick Van and Minibus Sales. If I tried to use it for Burnley Savings and Loans, I'd...

Let me guess. Risk going to prison? Got it in one. Why was it that every time I tried to move forward, there was some faceless authority threatening me with porridge for breakfast? I've always been of the opinion that it's often much easier in business to apologise after than to ask for permission before, but I figured that I probably shouldn't take that philosophy to extremes. I could apologise till I was blue in the face stuck in a prison cell, but it wouldn't get me very far. Time to get my thinking cap on again.

After a bit of research, I discovered that while it could take several months to get a *new* CCL, it was much quicker to amend an existing one. What if I were to add Burnley Savings and Loans to the CCL I already had?

More grave faces. More shaking of heads. I'd already applied for a licence in that name. There couldn't be two.

I was beginning to get jaw-ache from smiling in the face of these constant obstacles. These constant 'nos'. But like

I've already said, my job is to turn a 'no' into a 'yes'. I was determined to do just that. I went back to the drawing board and came back with another suggestion. If I couldn't add Burnley Savings and Loans to my existing CCL, how about forgetting the 'savings' bit – that had nothing to do with the Consumer Credit Licence, after all – and just adding Burnley Loans.

Finally, shaking heads became nods of agreement. A no became a yes. This particular backup plan was a good 'un. In my head, though, it was still just a backup plan. What I really wanted was the proper CCL with the proper name. And I wanted it sharpish. So I adopted the strategy of becoming a complete and utter pain in the arse to the Office of Fair Trading. I tortured the people there to death, ringing them every single day, making sure they had every single scrap of information they needed in double-quick time. And, hey presto, with a bit of encouragement it transpired they didn't need six months to send me a slip of paper after all. My new CCL came through in just four weeks – record time, or so I'm told. It's amazing what a little bit of nagging and sheer persistence can do...

The CCL is one of a number of documents that any bank has to have, whether or not they have a banking licence. There were certain other pieces of paper that I had to get my hands on too. One of these was a Data Protection Licence. Because we would, in the process of assessing – and hopefully approving – people for loans, be accumulating sensitive data about our customers. The Data Protection Licence was in place to ensure that we didn't disclose that information to anybody else. It would be vitally important that we stuck by the Data Protection rules because if we failed to do so, our CCL would be withdrawn and the job, not to put too fine a point on it, would be fucked. The bank also had to sign anti-money-laundering documents. This meant that if anybody came into the bank wanting to deposit a large quantity of cash, the onus would be on Burnley Savings and Loans to satisfy themselves that this wasn't, say, drug money, because as soon as it's deposited and then a cheque for the same sum is written out to somebody else, hey presto, dirty money might have been laundered clean. If the depositor couldn't show where the money had come from, then I couldn't touch it – and nor, to be frank, would I have wanted to. The Bank of Dave was there to help the community, not to help criminals launder their dirty cash. I found it interesting to learn that this is the case for all banks, and that even if they do accept a large cash deposit from one of their customers, if it's over a certain limit that deposit automatically gets reported to the Bank of England so that the relevant authorities can follow it up if necessary.

The purpose of the Bank of Dave was to be better than the other banks. I wanted to lend money to people that couldn't necessarily get credit elsewhere. But that didn't mean I wanted to be reckless with my lending. It was, after all, that kind of behaviour on behalf of the big banks that got us into this mess in the first place. If they had only lent sensible sums against assets worth more than the loan to people who were likely to repay them, they wouldn't have run out of money. My way of deciding whether or not a particular business or individual was likely to repay their loans was going to be rather different to the ordinary way – I wasn't going to have the Bank of Dave suffering from the 'computer says no' syndrome – but that didn't mean I couldn't use the same means that the banks do to assess whether a customer was a good bet or not. You've probably heard phrases like 'credit score' being bandied around; perhaps you've even wondered what yours is. I decided that it was important for the Bank of Dave to be able to have an idea of a potential customer's lending history if it was going to lend money in a sensible fashion. To do this, we needed the services of a company called Experian.

Experian is one of a couple of companies that supply details of individuals' personal financial history. You can go on their website any time and find out exactly what they've got on you. I think you'll be surprised. Your past addresses; your bank accounts; any loans you have and whether they're up to date; your electoral register details; any aliases you may have had in the past. The list goes on. Any financial institution who subscribes to this service has the ability to look up the details of anybody applying to them for a loan, and to base their decision on the information they find there. Perhaps you find it spooky that all your personal information is so easily available. However, given that the information is there for the lenders to examine, the more interesting question, it seems to me, is how do they choose to interpret it.

Most lenders will take one look at your credit score – which is a number between 0 (the worst) and 999 (the best) – and make their decision solely based on that number. To my mind, that's a blinkered way of doing business, because the credit score is only half the story. Somebody may have got into difficulty in the past – we all know that life can throw surprises at us – but it seems to me that it's not so important that they might have been in arrears in the past, but rather how they dealt with it at the time. Did they make a successful effort to pay the money back? If so, I'd be inclined to look favourably on them. Obviously if a potential customer was a serial defaulter with a terrible history of not paying money back, I wouldn't go near them – the Bank of Dave had a duty to everyone involved to lend responsibly. But the bottom line was that I only wanted the credit score to be one of the tools the Bank of Dave used to judge whether or not it was doing this. The other tool would be my old favourite – a good bucketful of old-fashioned common sense. You can tell a whole lot more by looking someone in the eye than by staring at a sheet of figures.

Linked with Experian was a service called AutoCheck. This would allow the Bank of Dave to run checks on vehicles or machinery against which customers wanted to take a loan. So, if somebody knocked on our door wanting a loan for a car, we could check the value of the vehicle in question, make sure the plates hadn't been changed or the chassis involved in an accident, and satisfy ourselves that there wasn't a loan already secured against it. In that way, we would be avoiding getting ourselves into the 'toxic loan' situation, whereby lenders lend money against assets worth less than the loan itself – it would, after all, be wildly irresponsible to lend someone £1,000 against a car that was only worth £500. If they defaulted and, as the last resort, we had to take the car back, we'd be out of pocket when we tried to sell it. And if the Bank of Dave was out of pocket, the community it was trying to help would be out of pocket too. Equally, we'd need to be sure that they hadn't already borrowed £1,000 against the car from somebody else, and to register the fact that we had first dibs on it if the worst came to the worst. It's not nice having to think about repossessing people's assets, but the Bank of Dave wasn't there to give out free ice cream. I would have a duty to make sure people were fully aware that they did have to repay the money, or else they would be compromising the whole enterprise.

I had the first component of the Bolt covered: with the Consumer Credit Licence and all the associated bits and bobs I was in a position to lend money responsibly. But as we know by now, lending money is only the half of it. I had to take deposits as well, both from individuals and from other companies. I had decided that I would match my depositors' money pound for pound, so that the fund we had to lend out would increase more quickly, but until I had deposit-taking facilities, I'd be matching zero pounds with zero pounds. Taking money from other companies didn't appear to be a big problem: the second component of the Bolt simply involved setting up a limited company of my own that allowed me to do this. Taking money from individuals, however, looked like being the fly in my ointment. A very big fly, if I'm honest, and a very sticky ointment.

That's not to say I didn't have a plan. I did. I hadn't given up on getting a full banking licence, but in the increasingly likely event that I was unsuccessful within the 180 day time frame I had set myself, I had decided that my next best route would be to try and set up what is known as a Credit Union. It was one of the very few ways I could see of legally taking small deposits from local people.

Credit Unions have a history dating back at least 150 years. They originated in Germany where, in rural communities, there were very few financial institutions to help local people with the essential services that the banks had started to provide. There were lots of reasons for this. The merchant banks in the big cities saw the cash flow of these rural communities as being too small and too seasonal to bother with, and they failed to see that the inhabitants of these communities had anything to offer a contemporary economic system. What they didn't realise was that there are different ways of measuring economic value. Ask a fancy sociologist and they're likely to tell you that all social networks – and I'm not talking about Facebook – have a value. They call it 'social capital', as distinct from 'physical capital' or 'human capital'. To understand what that means, think about a plumber. He's got a wrench in the back of his van. That wrench is physical capital. He's also got twenty years' experience of fixing people's toilets. That's human capital. Neither of these are any good to him if he hasn't got any toilets to fix, however. Fortunately, he lives in a small community where enough people have enough toilets with enough blockages to keep him in business. That community, therefore, has social capital. All communities have it, if you know where to look. The first rural credit union was created in 1864 by Friedrich Wilhelm Raiffeisen who understood all this, and within 25 years, the system had spread across Europe. It was not until the twentieth century that the credit union idea spread to North America when a Canadian journalist by the name of Alphonse Desjardins learned that a man from Montreal had been stung for just shy of $5,000 interest on a $150 loan – a reminder that there's nothing new about loan sharks out to target those who are struggling and unsuspecting.

In the UK, credit unions grew out of very similar institutions which had been around since the Industrial Revolution, known as the Friendly Societies. During this time, impoverished workers had very little in the way of welfare or protection – barely more than the limited Elizabethan Poor Laws. The Friendly Societies allowed the members of small communities to make small, regular payments that were pooled together in order to create a fund out of which insurance against emergencies or hardship could be provided, as well as offering services such as pensions, savings and cooperative banking. Many of these Friendly Societies were run along political or religious ideals; and as the name suggests, they did also encourage friendship, or community, among their members. Hard to imagine a modern-day bank doing that. Some of these Friendly Societies still exist, but they are generally unrecognisable compared to the original institutions, having mostly evolved into big, mutually-run insurance companies.

The original Friendly Societies evolved into Building Societies, which were originally small, temporary institutions in which the workers in a local community pooled their money so that they could build houses. These houses were allocated around the community by the drawing of lots; when everyone had a home, the building societies were generally shut down, though some of course became permanent institutions.

UK credit unions fulfilled some of the functions of both the Friendly Societies and the Building Societies. They encouraged thrift and provided low-cost home loans. They were community endeavours, intended to help the local working classes, rather than line the pockets of those involved with the big commercial banks.

So, what exactly are credit unions today? Times have changed since the days of the Friendly Societies and the original Building Societies. Communities are not so localised, and we have a welfare state intended to act as a safety net for those at risk of great hardship. The modern credit unions still maintain the ethos of their predecessors, however. They are local financial cooperatives whose main purpose is to encourage thrift in their members and supply credit to the local community at rates that won't, if you'll pardon the phrase, break the bank. One of the principal differences between a credit union and a bank is that a credit union is owned by the people who use it. It has to be able to operate profitably, but it isn't obliged to pay any interest other than what it distributes in dividends to its members out of any surplus money it makes. Its profits, therefore, are shared with its members and reinvested in the local community, rather than lining the pockets of the already wealthy.

A credit union was not, in all honesty, what I wanted the Bank of Dave to be. I wanted to be a fully-fledged bank, to show that there was a better way to do banking, that there was an alternative to the big, greedy, inefficient institutions that seem to have us all over a barrel. I wanted to pay interest like a bank, not dividends; and credit unions, being local organisations, were only allowed to take deposits from within a very limited area. If somebody came to the Bank of Dave wanting to deposit a few quid and they came from outside of that area, I wouldn't be allowed to accept their money. However, there was no doubt that these community-based organisations shared something of the ethos of my own plans. It seemed to me that I could use the credit-union set-up as part of my scheme to sidestep the need for a banking licence. It could be a useful component in the Bolt. Crucially it didn't require millions of pounds to set up; and it wouldn't take years to get it. Still, it wouldn't be instant – you don't just nip down to the local post office and set up a credit union. It could take months, even if I got the application in quickly and made a real nuisance of myself to get it through asap.

I decided to make the application, but in the meantime I still had the major problem of not being able to take any deposits. It was a potentially fatal blow to the whole endeavour. It wasn't just that I wanted to offer the local people of Burnley a better rate of interest on their savings; without deposits, I couldn't lend money; without lending money, the Bank of Dave couldn't make a profit; without profit, I was dead in the water.

There was, I knew, one other path open to me. A loophole I could exploit. It wouldn't allow me to take deposits from the man in the street, but it would allow me to build up the bank's funds so that I could start lending. There was a mechanism whereby I could take deposits from what are known as 'high-net-worth individuals'. You might think that's a phrase that sounds like it just means 'rich bastards', and you wouldn't be far wrong. In order to be categorised as a high-net-worth individual, you need to have an annual income of at least £100,000, or to have net assets of £250,000, not including your primary residence, or to have dealt in stocks and shares in the past – in short, someone going into it with their eyes open. As you can imagine, people with that sort of money are as rare as rocking-horse shit in the middle of Burnley, but I felt confident I'd be able to use my contacts among well-to-do local businessmen who *were* high-net-worth individuals in order to raise what I thought of as the Bank of Dave's stake. And as you know, I never squander my stake. Anybody who invested in the Bank of Dave at this stage would have to sign a form stating that they were aware that they were in no way covered by the Financial Services Compensation Scheme and that they had no right to complain to the FSA or the Financial Ombudsman Scheme. They would, in short, be trusting me to be as good as my word that I would pay back every penny they invested, plus interest, no matter what happened. If I couldn't find enough high-net-worth individuals to invest in the Bank of Dave, I'd have to put my own money in. It wasn't ideal, and it certainly wasn't what I'd set out to do. One glance at the paperwork my potential investors would have to sign would be enough to make most people run a mile. But I was being stymied by regulations and red tape. I wanted to be better than the big banks, but the powers that be were putting obstacles in my way. I was determined to overcome them, but in the meantime I was being forced down the high-net-worth individual/serial investor route simply in order to get the whole thing off the ground.

I won't pretend that this initial problem wasn't a blow, but I took some comfort in the fact that I wasn't the only bank to have started off this way. The TSB had similar origins, and I remembered Roy Ruffler saying that he had, at the beginning, lent out money that had been invested in his enterprise by friends and family. But I also had an even more famous precedent – none other than Barclays Bank. It was started by two brothers who initially raised investments from family and friends long before they began taking deposits from the public. Of course, I didn't want to model myself on Barclays or any of the big banks, but it encouraged me that if great oaks like Barclays could grow from the tiny acorns of individual investors, then perhaps the sapling that was the Bank of Dave might have a chance.

You'll remember that banks are built around the assumption that not all their customers would walk through the door at the same time demanding their money – in short, that there would not be a run on the bank. This was even more of an issue for a tiny bank like mine than it was for one of the big boys. If five hundred people want to withdraw all their money from RBS on a given day, it would barely be a blip on their computers. If five hundred high-net-worth individuals wanted to withdraw all their money from the Bank of Dave on a given day, we'd be stuffed. I needed a mechanism to stop this happening. That mechanism was a thirty-day notice period. If one of my depositors wanted to get their money back, that was absolutely fine; they just needed to send me a letter thirty days before they wanted to take it out. That would give me some warning of what to expect.

And what of guarantees? Well, without a banking licence or a credit union, I was unable to offer anything connected with the Financial Services Compensation Scheme. All I could offer was my word that I would pay back every penny, plus interest, that anybody deposited in the Bank of Dave. To back that up, I signed a personal guarantee to Burnley Savings and Loans, stating that if anything went wrong with the bank, I could be personally pursued by the authorities, and any money lost could be recouped from my assets. I would have to keep an eye on things, and make sure I always personally had sufficient ready cash to back up my investors' money. I could get too big for my boots. There would be no bailouts for the Bank of Dave. I wouldn't be going cap in hand to the taxpayer. I wouldn't be relying on handouts to get me out of a mess of my own making. I was taking on full, personal, financial responsibility.

I think that's the way it should be, don't you?

PART 2

B-DAY

If you're not from my part of the world, I wonder what you know about Burnley. Perhaps you have an image of riots, racism and poverty. If so, I'll bet my boots that most of what you've heard is bollocks.

The people who live here are proud of their town, and rightly so. Nestled among the Pendle Hills, Burnley is surrounded by some of the most beautiful countryside in the world, and populated by some of the friendliest people. I love these streets where I used to cycle my heavy old Grifter bike as a kid from morning till night (I always wanted a bunny-hopping BMX, of course, but somehow Santa never managed to bring me one). And though my childhood was poor, I'll always look back with fondness at the days of fishing minnows out of the river then using them to catch pike in the Leeds and Liverpool Canal, of playing cricket with my mates on the Hard Platts, of street parties and being part of one of the best, most tightly knit communities in the country. I hate it when people try to do the place down. More than once I've left my Ferrari in the middle of Burnley, roof down, doors unlocked and the keys in the ignition. It's still been there four hours later. Where else in the country would that happen?

But it would be impossible to say that Nelson, Burnley and Colne have not had their share of problems over the years and decades. I only have to listen to my dad talking about his Lancashire childhood to know that I'm just a generation away from real poverty. If you sat down and listened to the story of Dad's life, I swear it would make you cry: a story of a family so poor they had to drink out of jam jars and wear clogs. When he was a kid, his mum put him in a children's home for a few years. It was a hard, rough place. Dad loved it: there were clean sheets, clean pyjamas, three meals a day. For one of the poorest kids in one of the poorest parts of the country, it was luxury.

Mum and Dad grafted hard in the mills all their working lives. They might have been poor, but they gave us a very good upbringing, and were the most caring parents anybody could wish to have. Still, the tiny, terraced house in Nelson, Lancashire where I was born seems very distant from the country estate I'm now lucky enough to call home. Those days of not having a couple of quid to rub together are long gone. At least, they are for me. But for so many people in my part of the world – too many people, some might say – life can be tough. And yet the people who live here care deeply about their town. You only have to visit Burnley FC on a Saturday afternoon to realise that. The town's football club has the highest population-to-attendance ratio in the country; when they were promoted to the Premier League in 2008 the sense of pride that rippled through the town was something you had to be there to experience – not a bad achievement for a town whose entire population could fit into Old Trafford. I'm proud to have the name of my business emblazoned above one of the stands at Burnley FC, but trust me: it also makes business sense to have it there, because the football ground is the beating heart of a community that is proud of itself. I truly believe that this is a town of good, honest, hard-working men and women whose full potential could very quickly be realised if someone would only give them a chance. And while it has its problems, I refuse to admit it's anything like as black as it's painted. I'm quite sure that on any given night it would be far easier to find signs of trouble in Manchester or London than it is up here. People associate the town with the riots of a few years ago, but today you could walk through the streets all day long: I promise you won't see a single riot! What you will see is honest, decent, ethical men and women working hard to make ends meet. I don't think it's untrue, or chippy, to say that there is an arrogance in some people when they look at communities like mine. A smugness. They confuse poverty and lack of chances with laziness and ignorance. Nothing could be further from the truth. And that's why I was proud to have set up the Bank of Dave in the heart of Burnley and why, when it came to finding staff, I wanted to dip into the pool of talent from the local area.

The Bank of Dave wouldn't be giving jobs to a legion of overpaid bankers who would eat up any profit we made with overheads; I wouldn't touch those risk-taking traders – who expect annual bonuses of the size that would keep several Burnley families going for several years – with a barge pole. But the day-to-day running of the bank needed someone with more expertise than I had. Surround yourself with good people, remember? When it came to keeping the bank's affairs in order, I couldn't imagine anyone much better than David Henshaw, a no-nonsense Yorkshireman from Bacup. He's a plain-speaking, headmasterly type. He's also a football referee, but not any old football referee – he actually referees the refs. Put simply, there isn't much that gets past him.

When it came to the old-fashioned business of savings and loans, David had form. He joined the TSB as a tender eighteen-year-old, working for them for a couple of years before moving to selling unit trust investments around the north of England. After only a year of doing that, there was a credit crunch in the UK – an interesting reminder that the failings we've seen in the financial system aren't just a recent phenomenon. They're endemic. It hit David's patch hard: Rolls-Royce shut down a big factory and a load of people found themselves without work. If they didn't have work, they weren't likely to invest money in unit trusts, so David set up as an insurance and mortgage broker in Burnley. At the age of thirty he met his wife and decided it was time to get what he calls a 'proper' job. He became the area manager for a company specialising in hire-purchase and loans, and that's the business he's been in ever since.

I knew that David's wealth of experience was just what I needed to get my show on the road. With thirty-eight years of experience in the world of banking and finance – from 1979 to 1986 he was a manager for the Bank of Europe – I knew he'd keep me on the straight and narrow when it came to paperwork, if nothing else! I was pleased when, having approached him, he didn't tell me that the Bank of Dave was a crackpot idea that would do nothing but lose me money, and I was lucky that he was perhaps looking for something a little bit more exciting on which to spend his time. He admitted to me that, back in his late teens when he was working for the TSB, he'd had the opportunity to relocate to New Zealand. He'd turned it down, but always wondered what the future might have held if he'd just seized the day. If he didn't get involved in the Bank of Dave, a project designed to make such a difference to so many people, he'd always wonder what might have been.

There was another reason why David would be a very good addition to the bank's setup. I was aware that, in my eagerness to lend money to struggling local businesses, there was a risk that I would be too generous, agreeing loans because I *wanted* to, not because they were necessary sound investments for the bank. Normally in business I'm absolutely ruthless, out to make every single quid I can; with the Bank of Dave, I was trying to help as many people as possible. Ordinarily, the two don't sit comfortably together. Balancing the business side of the bank with the fact that I was here to help would be tricky. David's experience, I felt, would be invaluable. He had a feeling for what were good loans and bad loans; his first question on judging a loan application would always be: will they pay us back? Don't get me wrong – David is no hard-nosed Scrooge. Like me, he has the utmost respect for somebody who might have had money difficulties in the past but has managed to find their way through them. But if a sweet old lady came to him wanting three hundred quid to pay the gas bill and David thought she couldn't pay it back, he would be making sure the safe remained firmly shut, whereas I'd be itching to stuff the cash into her handbag. Mark my words, if David Henshaw had been in charge of the country over the last few years, we wouldn't be in the mess we're in now. He would, hopefully, be a tempering influence on me.

David would be staying very much behind the scenes – or, to be precise, behind the black screen that divided the front of my little bank from the back – processing applications, helping me make judgement calls on who to lend to and dealing with the thorny issue of those of our customers who fell into arrears, as some inevitably would.

I also needed someone to be out front, dealing with customers as they walked through the front door. In many ways, this person would be the face of the Bank of Dave. Chris Woods left university to go and work as editor of a local newspaper in Rossendale. When the funding got pulled from the newspaper, he found himself a job with a mortgage and insurance company in Padiham and worked there writing out mortgage contracts for four years, until they moved all their operations over to Skipton, leaving Chris without a job at a time when it was difficult to find one. Chris is a polite, friendly, bright, trustworthy lad. He's not a flash Harry; he's the quiet, reliable kind of fella you'd feel comfortable with when you walked into a bank. I was happy to give him the job.

As far as staff went, that was it. Roy Ruffler had told me to keep my overheads down, and I was well used to doing that in my other businesses anyway. Now the Bank of Dave had premises; it had staff; it had a safe in the vault and a cash machine in the front. The only thing it didn't have was any customers. Or money. But I decided to look on the bright side: I'd come a long way in the few short weeks since I'd decided to go ahead with the project. We now had 180 days to show that it really was possible to be both a better bank and a profitable bank; or maybe we'd fail miserably, in which case I'd doff my bowler hat to the bankers in the Square Mile, admit I was wrong, and shut up about the whole thing.

It was with David H that I sat down to work out what the Bank of Dave's rates were going to be. I had only one criterion – we had to be better than the high street banks. This much I knew: our loan rate had to be more than our savings rate in order for the bank to make a profit out of the bit in the middle. And although I wanted my loan rates to be as low as possible, I also didn't want to compromise the savings rate. I knew that it was the strategy of the big banks to make their spread – the difference between the loan rate and the savings rate – as big as possible; *my* strategy was to make sure *everybody* got a good deal.

Typical savings rates at the time were less than 1%. In many instances they were 0.1%. That's the equivalent of 10 pence interest a year for every £100 you have in the bank. It's a pitiful rate of return. Plenty were .05% – 5 pence for every £100. With rates like that, you might as well stick your money under your mattress after all.

At first, I had grand plans. I would offer 10% – a hundred times what the other banks were offering. But until I was able to sharpen my pencil and calculate the true overheads of the Bank of Dave, it was impossible for me to make a sensible decision. Now, though, I had my premises and my staff. I knew what my start-up costs had been and had a figure for my weekly overheads: £396. It was time to do the maths.

When you see loans being advertised by banks, finance companies or whoever, you'll probably see the words 'Typical APR'. We'll deal with the APR bit later. First, let's think what is meant by 'typical'. This simply means that not all the loans given on that particular deal will be at the advertised rate. Lenders decide what rate to charge according to how much risk they are taking. If you have a solid gold credit rating, you're likely to be offered the best rate; if not, you aren't. The word 'typical' also indicates that the APR changes according to how long you take the loan out for. I don't think that's generally clear to people.

I wanted the Bank of Dave's rates to be totally transparent. There would be two different loan rates, and that was it. I knew from the off that, if our savings rate was to be a meaningful amount, we wouldn't be able to offer loans quite as cheaply as they were advertised in some other places, but there was one crucial difference: we would be doing our best to lend the money, rather than our best *not* to lend it. The loan rates we finally decided on – 8.9% and 14.9% flat – weren't the cheapest on the high street, but they weren't even in the same ballpark as the most expensive.

I used the word 'flat' to describe these interest rates, and I want to be absolutely clear about what this means. In the case of the 8.9% interest rate, for every £100 a business or individual borrowed from the Bank of Dave, they would pay back £8.90 in interest over a period of a year. We were legally obliged also to present our interest rates as an APR, or annual percentage rate. This is different from a 'flat' rate because it includes any other costs involved in the loan such as arrangement fees, but also because it assumes that, if you borrow money for *more* than a year, you only pay interest on that part of the loan that is still remaining. The typical APRs for our loans were 17.4% and 29% respectively – a far cry from the APRs of several thousands of percent that certain loan providers were offering. The reason everyone has to present their loan rates as APRs is a good one: if there is a standard measure of interest, it means customers can compare the cost of loans from different providers and know that they are comparing like with like. A flat rate, of course, *looks* cheaper than an APR. But I also felt that it was simpler to understand. Borrow £100, pay back £8.90 a year, or about 75 pence a month, in interest, or about £9 monthly in repayments of interest and capital over a year. If a business can do something with that £100 that's going to earn them more than the 75 pence interest it's going to cost every month, it makes sense for them. If not, it doesn't.

Our loan rates were pretty keen, especially given that we were going to be bending over backwards actually to *lend* the money, rather than shutting the door in everybody's face. They could have been even keener, but that would have meant reducing the amount we paid our savers and it was important to me that we didn't do that. I found it almost insulting that the banks were offering interest rates of .1% while the bankers were still lining their pockets. I simply couldn't accept that it was impossible to do better than that. Given that I would be striving to lend as much as I could at 8.9% flat, my ideas of paying 10% interest were clearly over-ambitious. But surely 5% wasn't unreasonable? That would still be *fifty times* what some lenders were paying. And provided I found a way to take deposits from regular members of the public, I would be giving them a safe and generous way for their nest eggs to grow, rather than ripping them off, which some supposedly respectable institutions seemed to be queueing up to do. Paying 5% interest could make a real, positive difference to some people in Burnley. The more I reduced it, the less positive it would become.

I hoped that the loans and savings rates we came up with would offer a win-win situation for everybody. The loans would be affordable, the savings would be generous, and the bit in the middle would cover the bank's overheads and leave a bit over to plough back into the loans, self-generating more income, and provide some profit for me to give to charity at the end of the 180 days. I had no doubt that plenty of clever bankers would think my scheme laughably unachievable.

Well bollocks to them. I thought it could work, and I was willing to give it a try.

The opening of the Bank of Dave – or B-Day, as I liked to think of it – was an exciting day for me and, I hope, for everyone involved. A friend of mine called Ted Robbins had agreed to come along and cut the ribbon. Now, I know that if a big building were to be opened in London, there'd probably be some member of the royal family there to do it; but I couldn't imagine the Duke and Duchess of Cambridge popping along to open up the Bank of Dave, and up in Lancashire Ted's the next best thing! He's a big deal round here. Ted's best known for his part in *Phoenix Nights*, but he also has a daily show on Radio Lancashire which loads of people listen to. We've been pals for years. I knew that Ted's presence, if nothing else, would attract a bit of attention, and as you know, I'm all for every scrap of free publicity I can muster. There was more to it than that, though. I knew that Ted really believed in what we were doing, and although he offered to get me one of his other celebrity mates, it was Ted that I wanted, because that kept it real. He was local and he was behind the project. It wasn't just celebrity for celebrity's sake.

It was a big ask for Ted, though. He was filming in Benidorm, and had to fly into Manchester Airport that morning especially for the opening. We had it all worked out – a taxi driver would be waiting for him at the airport, would take him home to change out of his Benidorm clothes into something more appropriate for Burnley, and he'd be at

Keirby Walk in time for the 2pm opening. Any nerves I had were less to do with the opening, and more to do with Ted getting there on time. I was still at home that morning when I got a text from him: he was on the plane, everything was hunky-dory. Brilliant. I started to relax.

Minutes later, I got a second text. They'd turned the bloody plane around.

My heart sank. I knew, even as I read the text, that the local radio 2BR would be getting ready to set up their mikes outside the bank; TV cameras were being prepped (I've no doubt that TV cameras are a common sight in Canary Wharf, but in the centre of Burnley people stare at them like a spaceship's just landed); half the journalists in Lancashire were on their way. And all of them were expecting to see my mate from *Phoenix Nights* opening the Bank of Dave. If I couldn't even keep that one promise, I was going to look like a right tit. I was going to have a *Phoenix Nights* situation all of my very own.

I racked my brains for someone else I could ask to open the bank at such short notice. Nobody sprang to mind. Right, I thought. Next best thing: I'll get Nicky to do it. (She didn't know she was next on my list of candidates until well after the event, but like I've always said, it's much easier to apologise than ask for permission!) After all, she was coming anyway. She could always bring a pair of scissors…

I drove myself to the bank. A stage had been set up outside, with speakers and all that gubbins. But I couldn't feel excited. It looked like Ted wasn't going to make it, and the whole thing wasn't going to be as good as a result.

But then my phone jingled once more. It was Ted: his plane was on the move again! It was pushing it, but it was *just* possible he'd be there on time. I got Chris to get on the computer and start tracking the plane...

Nicky had brought down my suit and bowler hat in her car, but when the time came for me to get changed, I realised she hadn't included a tie. Obviously, I couldn't be a bank manager without a tie. Panic stations again. Trying to find a quality tie among the pound shops of Burnley is almost impossible, but I begged Nicky to see what she could do. In the end she managed to find something – it was a horrible pink colour, but beggars can't be choosers, and it would have to do. And I was less worried about the colour of my tie than I was about the arrival of Ted. He'd made it to Manchester Airport, but it turned out his taxi driver was a bit hard of hearing. Ted was struggling to get across to the poor lady that he no longer wanted to be driven home first, but needed to go straight to Keirby Walk; and in any case, it transpired that she could only take him as far as Accrington. I had to despatch Nicky to pick him up while I paced up and down inside the bank, pinstripe suit and bowler hat on, unable to see outside but aware that the crowd was getting bigger, not to mention increasingly impatient to see what was going on. I realised I couldn't wait any longer. Ted or no Ted, I had to get on to that stage and announce the opening of the Bank of Dave before everybody lost interest and went home for their tea.

I took a deep breath, stepped outside and flicked my bowler hat up my arm and on to my head. I instantly slipped into DJ mode, a relic from the days when I used to earn a few extra quid spinning discs in nightclubs: 'Ladies and gentlemen! Welcome along! Thanks for coming!' I told a few jokes, explained what we were doing – I don't remember exactly what came out of my mouth but it was probably enough not to get booed off...

And then, from the corner of my eye, I saw a figure approaching, dressed in the last thing you'd expect to see under overcast northern skies: sandals, shorts, summer shirt with a passport in the top pocket, padding up towards the stage with a big grin in his face. Ted was here! He stepped up to the microphone beside me, looking like he'd just walked off a Benidorm beach, and took over like the true pro that he is, sprinkling a bit of showbiz razzle dazzle on the proceedings, Burnley style.

The curtain went up; we popped champagne corks; I had my picture taken with my mum and dad who'd come down from the bungalow in Nelson where they still live. I think they were as surprised as anyone that the tearaway I was in my teens was now trying to take on the whole banking system; or maybe they were just used to me doing slightly crazy things.

You never know, when you start a new venture, quite how it's going to be received. But the day we opened the Bank of Dave, I knew I'd touched a nerve. Of all the passers-by who stopped to have a chat, there wasn't a single one who didn't appear delighted by the idea of taking the banks on at their own game. You can learn a lot about business by listening to the opinions and concerns of ordinary members of the public rather than the opinions of so-called experts, and they confirmed to me that day what I already suspected: there was a general feeling out there that the big banks had had it too good for too long. It was time for them to give something back, and if my tiny bank showed them up for what they were, everyone seemed to be behind it.

And it was on B-day that I first met Betty. You remember her? The widow whose savings had magically disappeared? Betty was very eager to deposit some money with Burnley Savings and Loans. I was prepared to offer her 5% interest – more than she'd get at any other bank – and I was prepared to take on all the risk myself. If the Bank of Dave made profit out of the money she deposited with us, all well and good; but if we *lost* her money, we wouldn't just be saying, 'Sorry, love, that's the way the cookie crumbles'. If we stood to make profit, it was only fair that we shouldered some risk: I would be personally responsible and would pay her back, interest and all, from my own pocket.

There was just one problem. I couldn't take Betty's money.

She was not a high-net-worth individual. She didn't earn £100,000 a year. She didn't have £250,000 in assets. These were meaningless sums to her. And as such, I would be breaking the law if I went anywhere near her nest egg. I *wanted* to pay her 5%. I *wanted* to give her a good deal after being treated so badly. But I couldn't. Simple as that.

And so, while the opening of the Bank of Dave was a good day for me and would be, I hoped, a good day for Burnley, it was tinged with more than a little frustration. I was able to do half of what I set out to do: lend money to local people who couldn't get credit from the banks. But for the savings side of the business, I still had a mountain to climb. I could take deposits from people who already had lots of money, and pay them their 5% without any problems at all. But all that would mean was that the rich would be getting richer, and that wasn't the idea behind my tiny bank at all. Far from it. I was stymied by regulations and red tape. My bank, I knew, wouldn't be a *real* bank – not in the way I wanted it to be – until the day came that I could take Betty's money.

And from what everyone around me seemed to think, the chances of *that* happening within my timeframe of 180 days were looking increasingly unlikely.

SHARK LOANS...

Let me tell you my approach to advertising.

Back in the day, when I wanted to learn how to be a DJ so I could earn a few quid at night, I needed to get the skills from someone who knew what they were doing. That someone was my best and oldest friend Sean Bannister. Sean agreed that if I helped him out with moving his gear in and out of venues, roadie-style, he'd teach me how to DJ. My main job for Sean was carrying the speakers. Now, these speakers were heavy and lugging them up the four flights of stairs at the One-Ten Club in Burnley was hard graft. But that was the deal: I had to carry the speakers if I wanted to learn from the best.

Years later, I had to carry the speakers again, but only metaphorically. I knew I needed to learn the business of marketing, so I hired a PR firm for a couple of very small jobs. I helped out as much as I could; and while I was helping out, I was watching and learning. Believe me, carrying the speakers is the best way of getting the know-how you need.

So what did I learn about marketing from that PR firm when I was carrying the speakers? Firstly, like most things in business, it's not rocket science. Secondly, you need to think outside the box.

Marketing is what sells your product. If nobody knows you have a car, or a cup of coffee, or a tin of beans, or a bunch of flowers to sell, nobody's going to buy it. Trouble is, advertising is very, very expensive. There's a reason big firms have their names round the edges of football pitches and in lights on tall buildings in Piccadilly Circus. But unless you're Coca-Cola, there's no way you can afford the kind of money that this sort of advertising will cost you. The likes of you and me have to be more modest in scale. But even half a page in a local newspaper is going to cost you hundreds of pounds. If you're Asda or Kwik-Fit, that's fine. But for most businesses, that would be all their profit from the goods they're advertising, eaten up already. Do the maths and you'll soon see it doesn't make sense.

There's another problem with that expensive half-page advert in the local rag. It might have a circulation of tens of thousands, but how many of those readers simply turn over a page as soon as they see an advert? Most of them, if they're anything like me. The best way to make someone read an advert is if they think it's a story. And stories, as opposed to adverts, have another advantage: they're free. But here's the problem: for your product to be a story, you have to make it sexy and interesting.

Now let's face it, there's nothing more boring than a minibus. I've learned the hard way that trying to make a minibus sexy and interesting is a tall order. The answer I've come up with is to stick a Ferrari or a helicopter next to it. You'd be amazed at how photogenic they suddenly become. If I can use the helicopter to fly in and visit a customer, suddenly it's a story, and people are far more likely to read that than to read an advert promoting 10% off at Fishwick's. Local newspaper journalists actively *want* to find stories to run. The same goes for local radio and even local telly. Your job is to give them that story on a plate. You'd be astonished at how many hundreds of thousands of pounds' worth of free advertising I've earned myself over the years by that simple method.

I'm lucky enough to have the toys that I have, and I'm fully aware that not everyone has Ferraris or helicopters to stick next to their products to make them interesting. It doesn't matter. You just need to think of something you can do that nobody else has done. Let's say you own a tiny pie shop. Business is flagging and you need a bit of extra footfall. You can't afford to advertise, and you quite rightly understand that there's nothing very sexy or interesting about your product: nobody's going to run a story that you're offering 15 pence off every meat and potato pie. So what do you do? Here's an idea: make the longest sausage roll in the north-west. Make it three times longer than any sausage roll anyone can buy anywhere. Or, sprinkle the pastry with a pinch of gold leaf, charge double and make it the dearest sausage roll in the country. All of a sudden you've got something to talk about. I can give you a cast-iron guarantee that any local radio station in the country will have you in to talk about it; you'll get a page in any local rag you care to name. Even if the sausage roll has cost you a hundred quid to make, it's going to earn you £5,000 worth of advertising. In fact, it's earned you more than that, because it's a story that people will read or listen to, not skim over or switch off. It is, as the old cliché goes, publicity that money can't buy.

I'm a bit further on in terms of PR than a lot of people. I sponsor an entire stand at Burnley FC. But a smaller business could do a similar thing on a smaller scale. Do ten minutes' research: I guarantee that there will be a kids' football team local to you who would chop their left legs off to have somebody come along with a batch of new shirts with a logo for your business emblazoned on the front. It'll cost you a hundred and fifty quid to have the shirts made up, and maybe another fifty quid for some shorts and socks. Hey presto: you've sponsored a local football team and that will guarantee you half a page in the local paper. Not only have you done something that makes a real positive impact in the local community, you've got yourself thousands of pounds' worth of publicity for practically nothing. And every time people see those kids play, they're reminded of your business. Your name's out there. I guarantee that increasing awareness of your brand will help you shift more pastry.

So, you've made a three-foot long sausage roll; you've kitted out the under-twelves in a brand-new strip; and you've reaped the rewards in terms of advertising. Don't let it slip through your fingers. Make friends with the journalists, and photographers, and editors, and radio presenters that you've met along the way. Send them a bag of Cornish pasties now and then. I can flick through my mobile phone and show you the name and number of every editor of every media outlet in my neck of the woods. I could phone any of them up and know that they'd take my call. Any time I think of something that might be of interest, I'm on to them. I'm still practising what I preach twenty-five years on. And it was for this reason that I tapped Ted Robbins up for one more favour before the bank went live.

Loans, as we've learned, are a bank's bread and butter. To you and me, a loan is a liability; to a bank, it's an asset. Loans earn them money, and if you've got this far in the story you hopefully understand why that's a good thing, so long as it's done responsibly. The Bank of Dave had its seed money; this didn't yet consist of deposits from local people the way I wanted it to, but my high-net-worth depositors were still expecting 5% interest, and this was money that the bank had to earn. I needed to start lending. I needed to let people know that the bank was open for business.

However, the bank could ill afford to pay thousands – or even hundreds – advertising its services in the local press. There'd be no ten-foot banners for the Bank of Dave at the local airports. I had to make do with what I had. And what I had was my pal Ted. Ted agreed to have me on his show to talk about the Bank of Dave and to drum up some interest from anyone in the area who needed a loan but couldn't get credit from the banks. Normally, Ted's guests have four or five minutes. I was on there for nearly an hour, giving it all my patter, putting out the word that we were open for business, which in turn led to lots of stories in the local papers.

And after that, it was just a matter of waiting to see who came walking through our door.

When a bank declines to give someone a loan, they'll come up with all sorts of reasons as to why they won't do it. They'll talk about credit scores and risk profiles. They'll pretend that their decision is nothing to do with them and everything to do with you. Here's how you can tell they're talking out of their arses.

Robert Ashworth is an accountant in Nelson. He and his partner had been in business for nigh on three decades. His partner had decided it was time to hang up his boots. It was going to cost Robert a certain sum of money to buy him out. He had half the money sitting in his bank account and he wanted to borrow the remaining half. His credit score was rosy. He had perfect books. Of course he did! He's an accountant! In buying out his partner, he would be entitled to *all* the profits from their little organisation. His profits were going to increase. And yet, his bank would not lend him the money. It didn't take much for me and David H to convince ourselves, having met him, that Robert was a proper person who I could be sure would pay me back. I agreed that the Bank of Dave would supply the loan he required, and his story highlighted to me exactly what people were up against. Because if an accountant, who's been in business for more than twenty-five years, who has perfect books and an impeccable credit rating, and who was more than likely to increase his profits as a result of the loan, couldn't get credit, then really: what chance would the local plumber or builder have? None. What about Geoffrey Aspin, a scrap dealer over in Blackburn? His is a simple, understandable, profitable business that involved taking parts off scrapped or damaged vehicles and selling them on. Geoffrey wanted to borrow a proportion of the money he needed to buy a small building as part of his pension policy. He had more money on deposit in the bank than he actually wanted to borrow, and still the computer said no. I told him I'd lend him the money if he wanted it. Chances were he might get it cheaper elsewhere in the future, and if he did he could pay me back at any time with no penalties. I like to think that was a weight off his mind, and these two simple stories, to me, were proof positive that the banks had simply stopped lending. There were plenty more.

I said at the beginning of this book that the story of the Bank of Dave isn't a story about a bank, or about a bloke called Dave. It's a story about people. It was only once the requests for loans started to come in, and I started to go out into the community to talk to real people with real problems in real businesses, that I started fully to understand the huge variety of hard-working, imaginative, entrepreneurial minds there are out there among the regular folk of regular communities. What follows is a small selection of these people. They are by no means the only individuals or businesses that the Bank of Dave ended up lending to, but I hope they'll give you an idea of just what might be possible if, instead of thinking of people as numbers on a spreadsheet, the bankers hauled their backsides away from their desks and their computer screens, and went out there to find out exactly what's going on at the grass roots. I think they might be surprised.

On the top of a hill just outside Burnley, there's a man who builds boats. They aren't just ordinary boats. They're works of art. And this Noah of the north-west is called Shaun. You'd like him.

Shaun's a joiner by trade, and a bloody good one. Three or four years back, he found himself on a job down in London working alongside an eccentric painter and decorator who didn't strike him as anything like the usual painter and decorator type. They got talking, and this fella, who was full of beans and full of stories, gave Shaun his potted history. He used to be a top salesman, he told Shaun, but it was a high-pressure job that took its toll on his life. His wife left him; he was burnt out. He decided that the one thing he'd always wanted to do was live on a narrowboat. So he cleared his debts, left his job, bought himself the narrowboat he'd always wanted, and the rest was history. Shaun was intrigued. He'd never met anyone who lived on a narrowboat before; it seemed like an eccentric choice for an eccentric bloke.

A couple of weeks after that, Shaun was doing a bit of scuba diving – one of his hobbies. He got chatting to one of the other divers, and it transpired that this chap worked on narrowboats. A month later he was on another job up north with a builder who'd just *ordered* a narrowboat. It was almost as if someone was trying to tell him something. He asked the builder if he might have a look at it – just the empty shell with nothing else in it at all. The builder was happy to oblige and took Shaun along to take a peek. He loved what he saw, and it got him thinking.

Shaun had enjoyed caravanning with his missus for years. He'd enjoyed tinkering with his caravans too. It wasn't just the joinery that fascinated him: he found himself obsessed with making his caravans as energy efficient as possible. And now he could see a way for his old interest and his new interest to collide.

It was a time of change in Shaun's life. He and his wife were thinking of selling up and emigrating to Australia, but having been out there a couple of times and really thought about it, the bottom line was that they both decided they preferred Lancashire. He really is a local lad to his fingertips, someone who just wasn't prepared to swap the rolling hills of the north-west for the desert temperatures down under. And so, having decided to stay around Burnley, and with the seed of an idea planted in his head, Shaun did what lots of guys do when they need a bit of advice: he turned to his dad. Shaun's dad, by all accounts, was exactly the kind of person to give it to him straight. If his idea of going into the narrowboat-building business was, in his opinion, a rubbish one, Shaun's old man would tell him so. He didn't. In fact, once Shaun had shown him all his costings and workings out, he said, 'Mate, I'll go half with you.' And that little bit of parental enthusiasm convinced Shaun he was on to a good thing.

Shaun did sell his house, but instead of using the money to emigrate to the other side of the world, he decided to plough it into his new narrowboat business. He truly was putting his money where his heart was. Personally, I find that kind of attitude inspiring. And I can't help but be reminded that it's people like Shaun who are the very lifeblood of small-scale industry in our country. It is also, of course, people like Shaun who are at risk from the economic situation we find ourselves in. I don't believe that there is a single bank out there that would allow itself to be inspired by Shaun and what he's trying to do. They just don't think that way, do they?

Up till now, Shaun's joinery workshop had been based in Nelson; but building narrowboats requires a fair bit of space. So, when the chance came up to move to an out-of-the-way hilltop outside Burnley, Shaun seized it. You might think, to look at it, that it's an odd place to build narrowboats. It's nowhere near the canal, and it's not like he's going to get any passing trade from potential narrowboat purchasers. In fact, it makes perfect sense: before setting up shop on the top of the hill, Shaun made sure that the trucks that transport his boats wherever they need to go could access the site; and as passing trade is hardly crucial for someone making narrowboats – most of his custom comes from down south, and most of it derives from advertisements in specialist magazines and websites – this out-of-the-way location that allows him to keep his overheads down is ideal. More than ideal: to me, it has all the hallmarks of a well-run business.

As I write this, Shaun's on his twelfth narrowboat. This

little Burnley business has customers from all over the world. When an Australian vicar called him up out of the blue, he thought someone was having him on. But no, he seemed to be on the level, and they exchanged a few ideas and drawings halfway round the world before the vicar from Down Under announced that he was happy with what Shaun had come up with, and paid a deposit. Shaun was gobsmacked that it was all going ahead; he was even more gobsmacked when the Australian vicar turned up unannounced outside his workshop on top of the hill one rainy day, having travelled all the way from Australia to Burnley to see his boat being built. The point is this: I know from experience that people can be sniffy about the ability of ordinary people from my neck of the woods running successful businesses. Shaun is proving that it's possible for the smallest of operations to be truly international. It's not just the domain of the big boys.

Shaun freely admits that it has been hard graft getting to the level of expertise he now so clearly displays. Him and his lads have gone through a steep learning curve as they got to grips with the ins and outs of boat-building, but I don't think anybody could argue that they've now honed their skills to something approaching perfection. The first time I stepped inside one of Shaun's narrowboats, I was astonished. They're like luxury yachts – smaller, maybe, but just as splendidly kitted out. There are big double beds, burnished wooden panels, state-of-the-art kitchens and bathrooms. I could honestly say that anyone in the world, no matter how glamorous, could live in one of these narrowboats being built on this unprepossessing hill just outside Burnley, and consider themselves to be in the most comfortable surroundings imaginable.

Shaun's narrowboats need to be super-duper and high-spec, because his customers are very demanding. The finish on the boat needs to be like the finish on a brand spanking new car. The paintwork needs to be perfect. Blemish free. You can imagine that in a busy workshop, it's difficult to achieve that kind of finish with all the sawdust flying around; but any work in progress can't just be left outside where it would be prey to the wind, the rain and the snow. Building a second workshop just to house the boat Shaun's making at any given moment would be prohibitively expensive, so his solution is to erect a polytunnel – essentially a long, tube-like tent that's normally used for growing vegetables – just by the workshop. The polytunnel protects the boat he's working on from the elements, and from the general dust and debris that's part and parcel of working with timber. It's a good, cost-effective solution to a problem.

You've probably guessed by now that I'm a fan of Shaun's little business. He's passionate about what he does; he makes his boats to high quality and takes pride in his work; he employs local people, who genuinely enjoy coming into work where there seems to be a fantastic atmosphere; at the same time he keeps his overheads low by not insisting on being somewhere more expensive than he needs to be. I don't suppose he'll be retiring any time soon – I don't suppose he'd really want to, as he told me he'd still be doing what he's doing even if he had ten million quid in the bank – but he's doing what he loves and putting food on the table for his family, and for the families of everyone he employs.

But, as with any business, there are issues. Predictably enough, they're financial. They'd be easy enough for the banks to sort out if they were minded to, but as we know, most banks seem to have forgotten the reason they're there in the first place. And the issues Shaun faces are typical of the issues many – indeed most – businesses face at some point or other.

Shaun had no shortage of punters wanting to buy his fabulous narrowboats. But the punters were having difficulty getting what were in effect mortgages to finance them. Clearly, if his customers started falling by the wayside, his business was heading to the bottom of the Leeds and Liverpool Canal.

Problem number two – and this was the problem I could really help him with – was this: he had just one polytunnel. Only having one polytunnel meant he could only build one narrowboat at a time. And while he had to be wary of the three-milk-round syndrome, it was clear that this was a barrier to him being able to expand his business.

Now, I don't know about you, but I don't think you have to be Warren Buffett to understand that the Noah of Burnley had a good little thing going on top of that hill. So when Shaun got in touch, having heard me on the radio advertising for businesses who needed a bit of a helping hand, I was keen to go along to his workshop, have a chat with him and see if there was anything the Bank of Dave could do to help.

Already, the fact that I was there, on the top of that

windswept hill, chatting with Shaun about his life and his business, was enough to get him thinking. He had banked with the same branch for nigh on twenty years and in all that time his bank manager had not once come out to see where he was, what he was doing, or show any real interest in his business whatsoever. Now, call me old-fashioned – I'd probably take it as a compliment anyway – but that doesn't seem quite right to me. How can Shaun's bank make any sensible decisions about him as a businessman? He confided in me that he was so peeved by this realisation that he went into his bank and brought the matter up. The response? 'Sorry, Shaun. We lost your number.'

Somehow, I think that if Shaun owed them money, they might have found it again, don't you?

Walking around Shaun's place of work, I thought back to the bank manager who'd sat in my office and tried to give me money I didn't need because he only wanted to lend it out to people he knew he'd get it back from. He should have looked a bit further. I knew that Shaun was a decent, honest, ethical person. I knew that if I lent him money, he would do everything in his power to pay me back. I didn't need to look at business plans or profit and loss accounts. I just needed to look the man in the eye.

Giving Shaun a loan for a polytunnel was a no-brainer. Giving credit to Shaun's customers was more difficult. The sums involved were large, and they would extend over long periods of time – maybe fifteen or twenty years. They were, in effect, more like mortgages. My bank was too small – a few loans like that would have eaten up the lion's share of the money it had on deposit, leaving nothing else for me to lend out to other local businesses that needed it. What should a bank do in such a situation? Lend the money for the polytunnel and then walk away, deciding there's no profit to be made from the other side of Shaun's business? Well, I daresay that's what some banks would do. They are, of course, missing the point. If I lent even a small amount of money to Shaun, it was in the Bank of Dave's interest to ensure that his business thrived. I wanted to take my cue from the old-fashioned bank managers, who would give advice and help out where they could. I might not have been able to put in a line of credit to Shaun's customers personally; but that wasn't to say that David Henshaw and I couldn't use our combined know-how to hunt around for other lenders that might. I suggested this to Shaun and he seemed happy as Larry with the plan. We shook on it. The deal was done.

I don't know about you, but when I listen to the news and hear all the doom and gloom about the economic situation, the numbers involved are so huge they start to get a bit meaningless. Are they talking about ten billion or a hundred billion? And how much is a billion anyway? With those sorts of sums being bandied around, you'd be forgiven for thinking that the amounts of money people want to borrow from the banks, amounts that would make a real, positive difference to their lives, are correspondingly huge. They're not.

In the process of setting up the Bank of Dave, I went to speak to a bloke from the Federation of Small Businesses. He was right behind what I was trying to do, and he urged me to remember that lending small amounts – maybe a couple of grand a time – to lots of different businesses was likely to make a much greater impact on the local community than lending larger sums to a few. But I wasn't in business for long before I realised that even smaller loans than that could be genuinely life-changing. After all, if you haven't got a hundred quid, then a hundred quid's all the money in the world.

Robert is a busker. It's not a hobby or a sideline; that's how he puts his food on the table, and more strength to him. He doesn't earn a fortune and I don't suppose he ever will; he's disabled, and he regularly donates a proportion of his earnings to a local children's charity. When he came through the doors of Burnley Savings and Loans, however, the bottom had just fallen out of his financial world. Why? What's the worst thing that can happen to a busker? Quite simply, his amplifier had broken down.

Now, there was no way Robert was ever going to get a loan from a regular high street bank, or indeed from anywhere, to replace that amplifier, but make no mistake: that broken-down amp was as devastating to his business as a fleet of knackered Boeings would be to EasyJet or a global shortage of tomatoes would be to Heinz ketchup. Without an amp, he couldn't busk; without busking, he couldn't eat. And yet he simply didn't have the spare cash he needed to replace the essential tool of his trade. It was an example, in microcosm, of the problems so many businesses face. People don't need loans because they're greedy, or have managed their money badly; in the vast majority of cases, they need loans just to keep their businesses ticking over. It seemed only right that my tiny bank should do what it could to help this one-man band. We lent him the money; he bought his amp; he's back in business. As I write these words, he has so far walked into the bank every week to pay the few quid he owes out of his busking money, as good as gold.

It's small, sole-traders like this for whom the credit crunch has been particularly brutal. Bigger businesses often have the cash in reserve to weather the storm, like I did when my customers stopped being able to borrow money to buy buses. Those with more modest incomes, especially those in my part of the world living one day to the next, simply don't. It's folk like this for whom initiatives like the Bank of Dave can be not so much a lifeline as a lifesaver.

A friend of mine called Jan has a lovely clothes shop in Barrowford called Scruples. He has a fondness for sports cars and for a long time now he's had his various cars valeted once a fortnight by a mobile valet man called Peter Wilkinson. Peter has always done an excellent job for a reasonable rate. Cold, raining, dark – it doesn't matter what the weather's like, he's there on time outside Jan's shop, and he always works his socks off.

At least he always did, until his van packed in.

A van is to a mobile valet man like an amp is to a busker. Without it, he's not mobile, which means he's out of a job. Peter had applied to his bank for a loan but, predictably enough, the computer had said no. Jan called me up to explain that, since he couldn't travel, he was having to give up. He gave me Peter's story – he'd gone through a divorce and his credit rating had suffered a bit on account of it. But he was a great lad and Jan would back him to the end of the earth, no matter what some faceless pen-pusher might think. Was there anything I could do? All he needed was a small amount for a van, and a little extra to buy himself a special valeting machine – like a glorified vacuum cleaner – for cleaning the inside of vehicles, and a generator to run it. If he could get these, he'd be up and running again even better than before. If not, his business – 'Bugs Away' – and his career were over.

I met Peter. I liked him. I *believed* he was good for the loan. I spoke to a couple of his customers, just to be belt and braces about it and make sure they were as glowing in their reports as Jan had been. I decided that the bank's money would be safely invested in the man who'd had nothing but bad luck and who'd had every door shut in his face. He was on the brink of having to sign on and now, thanks to us, he had a future. It epitomised, to me, what we were trying to do. And again, as I write this, he has paid every month, on the nose, and he's picked up extra work on account of his new machinery.

If the big banks – who had been bailed out to the tune of billions thanks to his taxes – had their way, our mobile valet man would have been out of a job.

Entrepreneurs are everywhere. You just have to know where to look, and to recognise them when you see them. I'm not just talking about the Richard Bransons of this world. There's the same entrepreneurial spirit in a young lad offering to clean his neighbours' cars for a fiver a pop on a Sunday morning as there is in a whole series of *Dragon's Den*. It's just a question of scale.

Steve the Shark Man is an unlikely entrepreneur. What's that you say, Dave? Sharks? Just outside Burnley?

That's right. Sharks. Just outside Burnley.

Steve owns an enormous pet store on a local industrial estate in Great Harwood. He has all sorts of creatures there. Lizards and armadillos of all different shapes and sizes; a long, fat python that slithers lazily in the corner of a glass cage; but his speciality is fish. Especially discus fish. Never heard of them? Nor had I, but I soon grew to recognise them: round, flat, bright orange and about the size of the palm of your hand. I honestly don't believe there's a single person in the country that knows more about breeding discus fish than Steve. If you want one of these little beauties in your tank, he's the go-to man. And he's passionate about them, like few people are passionate about anything.

I always find it interesting to learn how people end up doing what they do, and doubly so when I have my banker's hat on. A person's past is a good guide to their future – not in the way the banks think ('Oh look, he once missed a payment on his gas bill, let's turn the bastard down!) – but in a more human way. How can you make a judgement about someone without getting to know them, at least a little bit?

Steve's story, like that of so many others, is one of ups and downs. As a young man, his trade was groundwork, and he spent his days, like I had as a youngster, on building sites. There was a time in his life, in his late twenties, when he was truly on his uppers: divorced, penniless, in debt and living alone in Clitheroe. His brother gave him an empty fish tank, in the hope that it would amuse Steve's eighteen-month-old daughter when she came to visit. Steve had no money to do anything with it, so his mum took him down to the fish shop to buy him a pump and a couple of goldfish.

Not so long after, Steve was laying a patio for a mate of his who had a big old fish tank in his house. When it transpired that the tank wasn't going to survive his mate's renovation plans, Steve took it off his hands, along with all the fish and the gear that came with it. And part of the package was a book on discus fish. He started researching them in more depth. And the more he researched them, the more he realised that he didn't *like* groundwork any more. What he liked was discus fish. And when he read that they were the only tropical fish that could be bred on a commercial basis in Europe, on account of the prohibitive cost of the electricity needed for less hardy species, the cogs started turning.

Steve isn't the type to do things by half. Before long his empty terraced house was filled with tanks, and the tanks were filled with discus fish. The extension was chockful; the kitchen counters were covered. He soon reached the stage where he could give up the groundwork and sell discus fish for a living.

Things went from strength to strength. In the mid-Nineties he set up a little pet shop in Clitheroe; in 2003, now engaged to be married again, he was in a position to buy his current place – Aquascope – from the previous owner. Business was good.

To me, that's an encouraging story of a man picking himself up, dusting himself off and making a proper go of his life. It's the sort of story that never gets told on your common-or-garden loan application form, but it tells you more than any list of previous addresses or credit scores ever could.

It was seven years ago that Steve first had the idea of filling his showroom with creatures that were out of the ordinary, in the hope of turning the industrial unit where his business was housed into something of a tourist attraction – a place where people might bring their kids for a trip out, rather than just another run-of-the-mill tropical fish shop. He was doing all right at the time, but was just looking to expand a bit. He turned a large area of his premises into the 'Jungle Room'. He had a Cayman crocodile on show and a giant tortoise. There were snakes and spiders and lizards, piranhas and, of course, discus fish. From the sound of it, it was more like Belize than Burnley; it was also, clearly, a bloody good idea. If you have a shop, the most important thing is to get customers through the door. Steve's plan was to encourage families in to have a look at the croc, and encourage them out clutching Nemo, a goldfish bowl and a bag of fish food. With a bit of luck, the more people came, the more they'd tell their friends. Word of mouth is a crucial tool when you're trying to market yourself. If you want people to talk about you, you need to give them something to talk about. The Jungle Room was Steve's version of the three-foot sausage roll I told you about earlier.

And it worked. Steve would find himself down the local curry shop of a Friday night overhearing people at the next table talking about the Jungle Room. Coaches of kids came into the shop on educational trips. Families were queueing up to visit. Footfall increased, and so did his sales.

Unfortunately, there was a problem.

Jungle animals need jungle temperatures. In order to keep the tanks sufficiently warm for the croc, snakes and spiders, Steve's electricity bill increased threefold, and that was swallowing up his extra profit like a boa constrictor swallowing a mouse. The Jungle Room might have been increasing his turnover, but it wasn't doing much for his profit. And as we know, turnover is for vanity, profit is for sanity. The Jungle Room had to close.

Despite that disappointment, there's no doubting that Steve's is a good little business, and it ticked over quite nicely despite the closing of the Jungle Room. But when the credit crunch and the recession hit, like everyone, he started to feel the pinch. When people don't have a lot of money, businesses like his get hit hard.

So what do you do in a situation like that? Pack up and go home? Close up the shop, sack all the staff and become just another statistic on the news? Or do you put more energy into getting people through your door and spending a bit of their precious cash on your products? If I were a government trying to get a country on its feet again, or a high street bank trying to revive my own fortunes by reviving a flagging economy, I know what I'd be encouraging people to do.

Steve is like-minded. Moreover, he knew from past experience that if he could just offer the people of Burnley something quirky and offbeat, something they were never likely to see anywhere else, he could get the punters in.

The solution to his problems, he decided, was sharks. Black-tip reef sharks, to be precise.

The black-tip reef shark is most commonly found among the coral reefs of the Indian and Pacific oceans. Fully grown, it looks satisfyingly shark-like, and as it prefers shallow seas, its characteristic black dorsal fin is often to be seen breaking the surface of the water. It is, in short, everything you'd expect a shark to be. If you or I saw one of these creatures swimming up towards us on our summer holidays, it would be brown-trouser time. In reality, they don't pose a very great threat to humans. There are a few reports of them having taken a chunk out of a swimmer's leg, but that's mainly because they have poor eyesight and have mistaken a human for something more delicious, like a nice juicy squid. Your average kiddie doesn't know that, however. To them, a black-tip reef shark is Jaws 1, 2 and 3 all rolled together.

Steve's idea was simple. Use his considerable expertise to set up a tank full of sharks in the hope that local people would come to see them. It wouldn't be so heavy on the electricity as keeping all those reptiles in specially heated environments, and let's face it: who *wouldn't* want to come and see a shark in the middle of Lancashire? Stick a tank full of piranhas next to it, and surely it's a done deal!

Trouble was, black-tip reef sharks and flesh-eating

piranhas don't come cheap – it's not like buying a couple of goldfish in see-through bags from the local fairground. Steve had no spare money, and he knew what we all now know: the high street banks were being considerably less entrepreneurial than he was. He reckoned he could beg and borrow most of what he needed to house and care for his sharks from his suppliers and his friends. But he knew from the off that nobody was going to give him any sharks for nowt, and that – he hoped – was where the Bank of Dave might come in.

I'll admit it. When Steve first approached me asking to borrow money to buy sharks, I wasn't thinking about interest rates and repayment schedules. I was thinking: can I come to the shark shop with you? The idea was so off the wall that I found it almost irresistible. But I had to keep my business head on. I had to persuade myself that I wasn't lending money because it sounded fun; I was lending money because it would benefit not only Steve, but also my tiny bank. I knew nothing about fish, but there was no doubting Steve's expertise. What I *did* know about was publicity, and there was no doubt in my mind that in marketing terms, Steve's idea was solid gold. It was true that, if Steve defaulted on the loan, I was hardly likely to turn up and confiscate his sharks; but the sums involved were not so large that the bank was ridiculously exposed, and in any case my instinct was that Steve would pay me back. And why did I decide that? Because I'd spent time with him. I'd talked to him. I'd looked him in the eye. Steve was going about things the right way. He just needed a bit of a helping hand.

It was very important to me that the Bank of Dave should lend ethically. I'm not talking about tree-huggers and hand-knitted lentil bake, but I wanted to make sure that any money I distributed went to people who were thinking carefully about the wider consequences of their businesses. The welfare of Steve's sharks was a potential minefield. I wanted to be sure that they would be happy, comfortable and well treated. I needn't have worried. These sharks were going to live in aquatic luxury around Shark Island.

Shark Island is a chunk of live coral in the centre of an enormous tank, about five metres by three, which requires half a ton of salt to its three thousand gallons of water to bring it to the required level of salinity (black-tip reef sharks can only live in very salty waters, and they have to keep moving, otherwise they drown). Overhead, there are special heat-producing lights to replicate Asiatic temperatures. The tank is low enough for kids to be able to stand on a little platform and look down at the surface of the water, where they can experience the thrill of seeing the fins circling around. Crabs, snails, starfish, stingrays and other sea creatures live in and around the living reef; there are algae in the coral sand, creating a natural environment for the sharks to dart around. Steve has created a complicated natural filtration system that ensures any waste products are broken down into nitrogen gas just as they would be on the ocean floor and the water is kept crystal clear. These sharks are just as comfortable – if not more comfortable – in their Burnley digs than they would be in the waters of Indonesia. They'll be fed anything they might consume in their natural habitat, principally squid and cod, and it is feeding time that's the most exciting moment for any kids lucky enough to see it. Steve pours a few drops of squid juice into the tank. Within seconds the sharks sense it and are whipped up into a frenzy. He then dangles lumps of squid just above the water with a pair of feeding tongs. The sharks jump through the surface and grab it with their sharp, vicious teeth. Added to this, they can watch the piranhas tucking into a feast of raw liver. Now *that's* entertainment.

So what does Steve plan to do with all this extra footfall? Sell stuff, of course. With a bit of luck and a fair wind, there'll be a good chunk of kids walking out of his shop after their trip to see the sharks clutching a fish bowl and their very own real-life Nemo. There'll be sweets on sale – Steve's wife is a chocolatier, and plans to make little chocolate sharks – and Steve also has a sideline building cabinets, so the more people he has in the shop, the more people are aware of this other string to his bow. I think you'll agree that Steve is not short on ideas. He's just short on credit, and that is exactly the problem the Bank of Dave is there to address.

If I lend someone money, I want to make sure I get it back. The Bank of Dave isn't there to be taken advantage of, and neither am I. The question is: what's the best way to do this? Is it to send threatening letters and bully any struggling customers to the point that they're far more fixated on you than on making their business work? Or is it perhaps a bit more sensible to do what you can to *help* them? To give them a bit of advice? To pass on any tips or ideas you might have that could help them? To do, in a nutshell, what the old-fashioned bank manager used to do? They are, after all, your customers, not the enemy.

Franz and Mark are two brothers, though you wouldn't think it to look at them. They're as different to look at as they are in character. Mark's the bubbly one, the salesman; Franz is quieter, but he's got a good business brain in his head and you'll hear as much business sense coming from him as you will from any City high-flyer. Why? Because Franz and Mark have been at the sharp end of high street retail for most of their working lives. Together they sell furniture. Tables, bed and sofas – quality gear from a big warehouse in Accrington, at a price that's right for a community that's hardly flush with the kind of cash you need for a top-end three-piece suite. They've built up their business – Furnimax – from small beginnings in a tiny shop in Brierfield before moving to their current place. These premises demonstrate one of the biggest problems for businesses on the high street today. The reason they were able to set up shop here is because they've got a rent-free deal; and the reason they've got a rent-free deal is because it had been standing empty for a couple of years, since closing down as a superstore. The way things are at the moment, anyone who owns a business property has to pay rates on that property even if it's empty. I'd be surprised if the owner was getting much change out of sixty grand a year, just for the pleasure of having it stand there doing nothing. It's an eye-watering amount, and there needs to be legislation to change this state of affairs. If a property is standing empty, there should be a massive reduction in business rates. If you take an empty building and set up a business there, you should get free – or massively reduced – business rates for 6-12 months. It's common sense; but common sense isn't always that common.

Franz and Mark, however, managed to use it to their advantage. They went to the owner and offered to pay his rates in return for having the premises for a peppercorn rent for a couple of years; if, after that time, he found someone else who was willing to pay him the going rent, they'd move out; if not, and if business went well, they'd come to some arrangement. The owner bit their arm off, and the lads sank every penny they had into filling this big place with affordable furniture.

I don't know a great deal about the furniture business, but I soon learned that the margins are tight on less expensive sofas. On an item that costs £399, they might clear £90 profit. Compare that to a £1,200 sofa, on which they might make £300. Both sofas take up the same amount of space in the showroom; both cost the same amount to deliver to the customer. And yet they might make three times the profit from one than from the other. The question is, how do you get someone to buy an expensive sofa rather than a budget one?

The answer, of course, is credit.

There are certain products that people are used to buying with the help of a loan. Houses, cars, vans... and sofas. Think of all those telly adverts you've seen for furniture stores: 'Buy now, pay later!' '0% finance!' For most people, a big sofa is a major expense. Instead of forking out a thousand quid at once, it makes sense to spread the cost over a year or two, especially if it doesn't cost any more to do it. But when credit is hard to come by, it hits small traders like Franz and Mark hard. It has a direct effect on their bottom line, because they can only sell those products where the profit margin is smaller.

So the problem Franz and Mark found themselves up against was this: how could their little furniture business compete against the likes of DFS? How could they offer 0% finance on furniture just like the big boys do? How could they help the residents of Accrington buy more expensive, better quality sofas? How could they sell to punters who didn't have over a thousand quid burning a hole in their pockets, but might find ten or twenty quid a week affordable?

I'll let you into a secret: in most cases, there's no such thing as 0% finance. If anybody's offering it, it's only because somebody else, somewhere along the line, is paying the interest. Often, that'll be the shop itself. They've done the maths carefully, and worked out that they can afford to take that hit if it means selling an item with a bigger profit margin. There was no question of Franz and Mark ripping people off or taking advantage of them. They were proposing to sell good-quality items, some of which retailed elsewhere for getting on for four grand, for just over £1,000. The deal I came to with the boys was that the Bank of Dave would do what it could to lend money to their customers (assuming we could satisfy ourselves that they were good for it); the customer would pay me back the capital on the loan; Franz and Mark would pay back the little bit of interest. Even when the loan was taken into account, the boys would still be making a good deal more profit on these dearer sofas than on the less expensive ones; as they could offer interest-free credit, they'd be on a level playing field with the big furniture chains; the customers would be delighted with their new furniture bought on credit that cost them nothing; and the bank was making its own little bit of profit. It was a win-win-win situation.

The finance, though, is just one side of the coin. The lads also had to persuade people that they *wanted* these super-duper sofas in the first place. Simply putting the dearer stock in among all the less expensive sofas in their showroom didn't strike me as being a very good idea. All it would do, I thought, was highlight the difference in price and make people chose the cheaper option. Their best bet was make these better-quality products something to aspire to. My advice was this. Separate off a corner of the showroom and make it look stylish and upmarket. Put a nice bit of wooden floor down, and some oak panelling on the walls. Think of a posh name for your exclusive range of furniture, and design yourself a highbrow logo – perhaps a coat of arms. If you separate the dear from the inexpensive, it makes customers want it more. Believe me: Apple wouldn't have sold half as many iPhones if they didn't have retail stores that were slick, exclusive and designed to within an inch of their lives; and you only need to wander past the windows of some of the big department stores in London at Christmastime to realise they understand that retail is all about presentation. It's in the detail.

Franz and Mark did just as I suggested, devoting a whole corner of their showroom to what they dubbed their Charles Morgan Range (it just sounded posh!). It came up a treat and I was sure that people would be attracted to it.

I gave them other advice too. You'll recall my take on advertising: that, most of the time, it's just too expensive to be a viable option for small businesses, and that it's the canny businessman who thinks of ways of marketing his products for little or nothing. Franz and Mark have a couple of vans that they use to deliver furniture to their clients and, sensibly, the sides of these vans are plastered with a big advert for their store. So far so good. Trouble is, these adverts are only doing their job when they're out and about; when they're parked up outside the store, the only potential punters who are going to see them are the ones already walking in.

Just down the road, however, there's a big Asda with a big car park, and there's nothing to stop Franz and Mark sticking their vans in that car park when they're not in use. Now that's what I call free advertising: to put a couple of billboards up would cost them hundreds, even thousands, of pounds a week. To park their vans costs nothing, and in a supermarket car park there's a huge volume of shoppers passing through every day. It's perfect exposure.

And the icing on the cake? For forty quid a day, Franz and Mark could hire a young lad to don what's got to be the best – and cheapest – mobile advertising device ever designed:

a sandwich board. And, in a stroke of genius, they gave him a rubber, Spitting Image-style Ali G mask to wear. He looks quite ridiculous, of course, and plenty of people give him plenty of stick. The one thing almost nobody does, however, is ignore him. The lad walks around outside the entrance to the Asda car park, pointing anyone who asks him in the direction of the furniture store. So now, half of Accrington knows about Franz and Mark's shop, and a fair proportion of them are in a position to buy a nice new sofa on 0% finance. You don't have to have an MBA to know that's the kind of thing that gets economies moving.

Ta very much, Ali G. And ta very much, Bank of Dave.

Franz and Mark are a great example of how the old-fashioned style of bank managing can make a difference. My hunch is that people in business don't want their contact at a bank simply to be a voice at the end of the phone, a blank face sitting in a call centre somewhere with no real understanding of what their businesses are or the challenges they face. In the old days, a bank manager would not only know his clients personally but would, so far as it was in his power, give them advice and help them run their businesses profitably. I'd done a bit of this with Franz and Mark, but it's fair to say that they already had good business heads on them. What about those people who are very, very good at what they do, who are hard working and enthusiastic, whose business has potential but who just need a bit of guidance to get them on the right track? How are such people expected to thrive now the days of more personal bank managing are at an end?

I'm thinking, in particular, of Christine and Keith. They run a tiny cafe in Sabden called Sandwitches, in honour of the local history surrounding the Pendle Witches. It's a homely place, not much bigger than the average front room, serving delicious, homely food. Christine and Keith, who are in their early sixties, are just about the nicest people you could hope to meet. They've worked hard all their lives, and now they want to employ an apprentice from Burnley College, not as a money-making exercise, but simply because they want to pass on what they know about cooking. They want to teach. They want to give something back.

Christine is a dab hand at preparing food on a larger scale. As well as running the cafe, she caters for twenty or twenty-five people of an evening; and she does all this at home. There just wasn't enough room in her little kitchen, so they turned their garage into an extra one. But everything was getting a bit old. The Aga is starting to break down and they need a new refrigeration unit, hot plates and gas rings. Their tiny kitchen also needs new worktops, because Christine simply didn't have the space to prepare all the food for the cafe and for her other catering engagements. Forget about swinging a cat – there wasn't even enough room to peel spuds, so they had to go outside and do it in a bucket. It was absolutely clear that she couldn't carry on working in this way. Down at the cafe they need a proper catering toaster and a new oven. They had been to the banks to ask for a loan for this, but it was the usual story. When I talked to them about their situation, they were at once disarmingly honest and anxious. 'David,' they told me, 'you are our last hope.' If I didn't do something to help, it was all over for them.

Christine and Keith needed money. But they didn't *just* need money. They needed advice. If they were to take on an apprentice, and earn the extra few quid necessary to pay back a loan, they needed to think about how to generate some extra income. From my point of view it was neither desirable nor ethical to lend them money without giving them whatever help and advice I could about how to give their enterprise a jump start. And so I started to educate myself about the business. And how did I do that? By spending plenty of time in their little cafe, eating their food, watching and talking to their customers. Doing, in short, what I think a bank manager *should* be doing.

The conclusion I came to at first was probably not what they expected – or wanted – to hear. The problem, so far as I could tell, was that their food was *too* good. They were investing so much time and money in it, that it was nigh-on impossible to make it as profitable as it needed to be. The last thing they wanted to do, of course, was lower their very high standards. This little cafe of theirs wasn't a profit-at-any-cost money-making machine; it was a labour of love. So it seemed to me that the only other options open to them were to find a market that would pay that little bit extra for food of a higher quality; and to get the word round the local community that Sandwitches was the place to go for quality food.

I could see them looking crestfallen even as I spoke. They had no spare money to advertise, they told me, and no experience of marketing themselves. But I explained to them my theory of advertising. We started tossing ideas around, dreaming up imaginative and newsworthy food items they could invent. What about a witch's brew, or a Pendle Witch Pie? Something different and interesting. I knew all the journalists and photographers — I could bring them all in and Christine and Keith could earn themselves thousands of pounds worth of free publicity. And when the story's been and gone, we could get the photographs back and turn them into a professional brochure. And they could make samples of their delicious food, and I'd go with them round local business parks looking for businesses who perhaps do conference meals, or lunches in their offices, and are willing to pay a little bit extra for something that isn't just a round of egg and cress sarnies. Them and me, guerrilla marketing, drumming up business the old-fashioned way. The more we got thinking about it, the more possibilities seemed to open up. I could see Christine and Keith becoming visibly excited at the prospect.

Christine did her research. She found out that at the Great Assembly and Feast at Malkin Tower at the time of the Pendle Witch Trials in 1612, a dish made of lamb, beef, bacon and spices was served. She adapted this into a delicious pie that she dubbed Malkin Pie. The couple made up posters advertising it, and as I write this, they are hoping to encourage local hotels and restaurants to start selling it, and I've no doubt it will be a massive hit. With a loan from the bank, they've turned their tiny home kitchen into a much better place for Christine to work.

Once Christine and Keith started thinking in this way, there was no stopping them. When Keith found out that there was some construction work about to start up the road, I suggested he take a few bacon butties, a pot of tea and some copies of the *Sun* for all the builders on the first day and try to persuade them to come up to the cafe for their breakfast and lunch. I could see his face light up at the idea. All of a sudden they were thinking like business people, and I didn't doubt that they'd soon see the benefit of it.

I truly believe that advice and encouragement like this is as important to people like Christine and Keith as the loan that's going to keep them afloat. I couldn't just hand over the cash and expect everything to be hunky-dory without offering them a bit of support. Are the big banks – the very institutions who have a vested interest in the businesses they should be lending to – ever going to go back to this way of doing things? Well, we can hope. But let's not hold our breath, eh?

Decent, ethical, honest people. From the start, it has been my conviction that these words describe so many members of my local community who are getting such a raw deal from the banks. They don't come much more decent, ethical and honest than Rachel McClure, owner of a small florist in Oswaldtwistle. She's jovial, bubbly and straightforward. You'd trust her even if you didn't know that before becoming a florist, she had trained both as a teacher and a social worker.

I won't tell you who Rachel banks with. Suffice to say that it isn't one of the big four, with one of whom she'd had dealings in the past. And I won't tell you the real name of her bank manager, not least because Rachel has only good things to say about her. We'll call her Jackie. When Rachel took a call from Jackie one morning, she was understandably anxious. She'd had bad experiences in the past with phone calls out of the blue from bank managers, and her first thought was that there must be a problem with her account. Maybe a payment hadn't gone through properly; maybe she'd slipped into the red.

It was nothing like that. Jackie explained that the bank had a new initiative. They wanted their managers to spend at least two days a year working alongside their customers and in their businesses. That way, they could get a better understanding of their customers' financial needs and issues. Instead of only knowing what it's like to sit behind a desk in a bank, they would gain some real-world understanding of what it's like to run a small business.

Sounds like a good idea, right? Sounds like the sort of thing a bank *should* be doing? I agree. Jackie came out to Rachel's florist's shop one busy Friday when she was preparing the flowers for a large local wedding. She got her hands dirty: dealing with customers, answering the phone, arranging the flowers, sweeping up. She wasn't just sitting in the corner with a clipboard; she was grafting like any other employee, and by her own admission she was surprised by how hard the work was. Jackie went back to her desk with a much better idea of the challenges her client's business faced on a day-to-day basis, and that could only be a good thing.

Now, I'm not here to tell you that Jackie was wasting her time. From what Rachel has told me, I've no doubt that she's an excellent manager, with every intention of putting what she learned from that day in the florist's shop into action, so that she could help the bank help Rachel, to the mutual benefit of both. Sometimes, though, the best intentions of individuals aren't enough, not when the faceless corporations for whom they work don't back them up. Was the bank's insistence that Jackie spend a day with Rachel borne from a real desire to 'understand her business better'; or was it a cynical marketing ploy, a way of polishing their crooked halo without having to do much to back it up? I'll let you be the judge of that.

In the wake of Jackie's visit, her bank issued a press release about this fabulous initiative that made them look so concerned and caring. And they earned themselves some good publicity out of it – magazine spreads bigging up not only Rachel but also the bank, with cheery photos of Jackie holding up an enormous bouquet of flowers in one hand and a cheque book in the other.

The proof of the pudding, though, is in the eating.

Rachel has owned her little florist's shop for eight years now, and the truth is it's looking a little tired. The shop next door has had the front renewed, and the difference between the two premises is noticeable. One has brand-new paintwork, cleaned-up brickwork and fresh pointing; the other doesn't. We've already seen in the case of Franz and Mark's furniture shop that good presentation is essential in retail; for a florist it's doubly important. If you're choosing somewhere to provide the flowers for your wedding day, you're much more likely to select a shop that takes pride in its appearance; and the impulse buyers that are so important to floristry as a whole are massively more likely to walk in for a bunch of daffs for the missus if the flower shop looks bright and appealing. I don't suppose you or I need to spend a day with Rachel to realise that.

So it makes perfectly sound business sense for Rachel to want to renovate the front of her shop. She didn't want to throw money at it. She just wanted to give the place a bit of a makeover and, hopefully, attract a few more customers in doing so. That's what her business needed.

And so she applied for a fairly substantial loan to cover the cost of the works. Bear in mind that the bank had already benefitted massively from the publicity surrounding Jackie's visit; bear in mind that they were trumpeting their new-found understanding of the needs and challenges of Rachel's business. You'd think they'd be only too happy to lend her the money, wouldn't you?

Predictably enough, they turned her down.

This is the very opposite of a risky loan. Rachel owns the premises she wants to maintain, and has a good chunk of equity in it – substantially more than she wanted to borrow. This means that, if the worst happened and she *did* find herself unable to pay back the loan, the bank would have that property as security. She runs a nice, profitable little business. She works hard and has roots in the local community. She's not going anywhere. She's not fooling anyone. She takes pride in her business and she's doing her best to keep it thriving in a difficult economic climate. How ridiculous that an industry which risked so much in such a reckless fashion, should think of her as being a bad bet.

As the representative of the Bank of Dave, I spent some time in Rachel's florist's shop too. I learned how to tie a bouquet of roses (not something we rough, tough men of the north are used to doing, let me tell you). And while I was with Rachel I noticed something important. It didn't matter to her that I had telly cameras following me around, as I did at the time. It didn't matter to her that I was the bloke who might lend her the money she needed. When a customer walked through the door of that shop, everything else became irrelevant. For the time they were in her premises, Rachel's customers were the most important people in her world. And that's how it should be.

I lent her the money she needed. What was more, I lent it to her as a personal loan without any security because I knew she would pay me back. Deal done. As I write this, she has so far never failed to make a repayment. And I'll let you into a little secret. If Rachel, or Steve the Shark Guy, or Franz and Mark, or the Noah of Burnley, or Peter the Valet Man failed to pay me back, there's no doubt that I would have to pursue them for the money. But deep down, I wouldn't see it as being their fault; I would see it as mine for making a bad judgement, and the wrong call. And that, I suppose, goes to the heart of the matter. The banks, so far as I can see, don't consider themselves responsible for what has happened. It's not their fault. It doesn't take a brain the size of a planet to work out that's bollocks. And if any bank is going to start to win back the trust of the public, they need to start taking responsibility for their actions. That's what my tiny, tiny bank was trying to do.

And so far, it was working well.

...AND LOAN SHARKS

I like businesses to be simple. That doesn't mean they have to be small, or cheap. One of the best, and biggest, businesses in the world is Coca-Cola, and the reason it's so good is because it's so simple.

They have one great product that has a big moat around it, by which I mean to say that nobody can get close enough to them to come after their business. They don't need to change or improve their product, and it doesn't cost them much to make. I'd be astonished if the production costs of a glass of Coke are more than a penny; the rest of the company's expenses go on advertising, and on making sure that nobody forgets about the brand. They are geniuses when it comes to marketing. Plenty of people have tried to take a chunk out of Coca-Cola's business. Nobody has ever come close. Coca-Cola is one of the most profitable companies in the world, and they're just too big to go after. Now, obviously I'm not suggesting that every company the Bank of Dave invested in should be Coca-Cola; but it should be simple and understandable. And there's no shortage of small businesses out there in our local communities which fit those criteria.

Some businesses, though, just don't stack up, and my tiny bank was in no position to dish out money to people I thought couldn't pay me back. That wouldn't be helping them, the bank, my depositors or those businesses that I knew could thrive if they could only get a bit of a helping hand. I wanted to challenge the banks' refusal to lend, but I also had to make sure I didn't fall into the trap that had ensnared them when times were good, and lend too much.

That meant turning people down. It wasn't something that came easily.

In business, I'm as ruthless as anyone. I'll haggle you down to the very last penny, sometimes more out of pride than out of financial necessity. With the bank it was different. I *wanted* to help people. More than once, David Henshaw and I found ourselves disagreeing about whether we should approve a certain loan, David always erring on the side of caution, and me on the side of generosity. Some prospects, though, were just too dotty even for me.

It's not that they weren't sincere. One lady – a Native American – thought she and her partner, an out-of-work architect, had hit on the most fantastic money-making idea, and she was looking for someone to lend her quite a substantial sum so that she could continue developing it. They were lovely people: genuine, friendly and eager to make a success of their idea. I liked them very much. I just didn't like what they had to offer. Her invention was a dog toy. The idea was that you strap it on to Fido's body, and some plastic gizmo suspended over him makes him run around and exercise so that you don't have to take him for a walk. She'd been to a dog psychiatrist to verify that her contraption wasn't harmful or cruel for the dog in any way, and had been given the all-clear. But I can't honestly say that her dog looked particularly happy as it demonstrated this amazing labour-saving device. It just looked like it was trying to get the thing off. Or maybe it was just jumpy because there wasn't a lamppost in the vicinity.

This woman's own bank had requested that she produce a projected business plan and, in good faith, she had obliged. She had forecast that if a certain number of stores (hundreds) took a certain number of units (hundreds), she would make a certain amount of money (hundreds and hundreds). Fine, except nobody had actually given her an order yet. The closest she'd got was with a couple of the big pet stores who had said that if she developed it, they might have a look. I told her what I've already told you: that a business plan can be scribbled down on the back of an envelope in seconds. She looked a bit perplexed, so I showed her. I drew a little graph, with 2011 at one end, 2012 at the other, and running between them a nice steep line forecasting that I was going to earn a million quid. It was, of course, not worth the paper it was written on. No business plan is. They're just a projection. A prediction.

I knew that I could not, in all honesty, lend a single penny from the coffers of Burnley Savings and Loans to support a venture like this. As much as I liked the couple, I didn't believe in the product. I knew, as sure as eggs is eggs, that I wouldn't see the money back. And although I didn't know what sort of response she'd have got from *Dragon's Den*, I *did* know one thing for sure: I was out.

Another guy wanted some money to buy rickshaws. If you live in London you might have seen these fellas taxiing tourists around the capital using pedal power. I was intrigued, but David H and I both agreed that the figures didn't stack up; moreover I couldn't really get my head around the business, and how it was going to make the kind of money it needed to pay back the massive investment – they wanted £70,000 for these futuristic pedalling machines. If I can't understand something, how can I make a sensible decision about whether to plough my depositors' money into it?

There are business loans, and there are personal loans. They are very different animals.

David Henshaw, with his years of experience, was instinctively wary about dishing the bank's money out in the form of personal loans, and I could understand why. If somebody is borrowing money for their business, they have a means of generating the income necessary to repay the loan. Personal loans are a bit riskier. They might be taken out in order to purchase a large item that is unmanageably expensive in one lump sum – a car, perhaps, or one of Franz and Mark's sofas. That's potentially OK, because then the loan is secured against the car or the sofa. These are items people don't want to lose, and so they have an extra impetus to keep up the payments. But the unsecured personal loan is a tricky one. Once it's spent, it's spent. Often the borrower has nothing to show for it, and they're in no better position at that stage to raise the money to pay it back than they were before they took out the loan. David H, knowing the pitfalls of lending money on such a basis, was reluctant for the Bank of Dave to burden itself with that kind of potential loss.

I thought differently. Although I'd had a remarkable lack of success so far, I was still desperately trying to find a way to take Betty's money, and the money of ordinary people like Betty. It seemed only right that, on the flip side, I should be lending out to ordinary people. Not business-owners and entrepreneurs, but those who – in no small measure because of the situation the banks' insatiable greed has got us into – were struggling in their day-to-day life. I wanted to be a bank, not a bog-standard finance company. That meant doing all the things a bank was supposed to do. And *that* meant unsecured personal loans.

There's no doubt that there was a crying need for short-term personal loans at a reasonable rate. You're probably aware of the controversy surrounding what have come to be known as payday loans – 30-day loans designed to cover an individual's shortfall until they next get paid. These are inherently quite risky loans, and I suppose it's understandable that anyone giving them might want to charge a higher rate of interest to account for the fact that they're likely to get more people defaulting than usual. However, the kind of interest rates some of these lenders charge would be funny if they weren't so serious. APRs of more than 4,000% are typical, and stories of people borrowing £500 and ending up having to pay back several thousand aren't uncommon. In my book, that's not profiting. That's profiteering. And the effect that this loan-sharking has on ordinary people can be devastating.

A young woman had fallen victim to just that kind of loan. A small debt had ballooned thanks to an APR of almost 3,500%. What does that mean in real money? If you borrow £10 for a year, you'd have to pay back £350. You don't have to be Carol Vorderman to work out that it's all too easy for someone on a low wage to end up having more interest slapped on them every month than the payments they are able to make. It's called a spiral of debt, and once you're in it, it's unbelievably difficult to get out, because it gets bigger, not smaller. The human consequences can be devastating. Houses lost. Families ripped apart. And because the people who take out these payday loans come from exactly the demographic that is least likely to qualify for credit from more reputable lenders, their chances of breaking out of these spirals of debt are correspondingly smaller.

This lass regretted having taken out a payday loan. That much was obvious. She was now in a situation where it would cost her £110 a month to pay off just £20 of debt. And in a depressed area like Burnley, £110 is a lot of money to find. And what makes things worse is this: when she told her payday loan company over the phone that she wanted to pay off the whole debt with a loan from us that was more than ten times cheaper, they tried to persuade her not to. They had no interest in trying to help her get out of this spiral of debt in which they'd landed her in the first place. They just wanted to keep on taking her money. Nice.

I'm sure there are plenty of people who would criticise her for taking out such a loan in the first place. But here's the thing: she's not a financial expert, and she's not rich, but loans of the type she took out are even now being marketed directly at people in her situation. I don't think that's right. I wanted my bank to help her out.

I know what you're thinking. How could we judge which of these people would be likely to pay us back and which weren't? If these people had got themselves into debt they were struggling to repay in the first place, how could we be sure that they weren't going to default on Burnley Savings and Loans? The short answer is that we couldn't. Not entirely. But, like the banks, we had credit-searching facilities, and it would be wrong of me to suggest that we didn't make use of them. If an individual or a business was up to their neck in CCJs (County Court Judgments, a legal claim for you to repay a debt) and was obviously a bad payer, we wouldn't touch them. If their credit score was good, their loan was more likely to be successful. But for the borderline cases, I would have to rely on my own intuition. I'd have to look the prospective borrower in the eye, listen to their story, and decide for myself if they were going to pay me back. I was applying the same criteria to individuals as I was to businesses. But I suppose it was to be expected that my first ever default was to be on a personal loan.

It was a textbook story: a young woman asking for a few quid to tide her over. It wasn't a massive sum, but then nor were any of the personal loans to which we agreed. Nevertheless, the woman failed to make her very first payment, and alarm bells started to tinkle in the Bank of Dave.

I was lucky to have David H's know-how. He explained to me that it's not uncommon for there to be a problem with the first payment. The standing order may not have been set up properly; there might be some technical glitch. And so he set up a system, and we followed that system in the event of our first ever default. David gave it two working days for the money to hit our account. When it didn't, he left the woman a phone message and a text message, explaining that her account was in arrears and asking her to get in touch. It's vitally important in a situation like this for the lender and the borrower to speak. If they don't speak, they can't resolve the situation. Normally, if it is just a clerical error, the borrower will be in touch immediately they get the message, eager to sort things out. But in this instance, there was radio silence. The tinkling alarm bells grew a bit louder.

David is nothing if not dogged. He managed to get hold of the woman on the phone. The explanation she gave for being in arrears was enough to melt the stoniest heart. Life was not going well for her. She'd been attacked, and had lost her job. It's not easy to pull the wool over David's eyes – he's been in the finance game for too long, and there's barely any excuse he hasn't heard – and he believed what she was telling him. It was a Friday when they spoke; she said she would get the money off her mother and come to the bank on the Monday to pay her first instalment.

Monday arrived. The money didn't.

David called again. The woman said she had the money, and would bring it in on Tuesday.

Tuesday arrived. The money didn't.

It was becoming a problem. What should I do? It was the bank that had taken the risk in the hope of making a profit. Hadn't one of my beefs with the big banks been that they'd been happy to pocket the profits when times were good, but were unwilling to take the hit when times were bad? My inclination was to write the debt off. Put it down to experience. David H took an alternative view. If we wrote off the few quid as easily as that, there were two problems that he could foresee. Firstly, the good work that Burnley Savings and Loans was trying to do would be directly compromised. Secondly, there was a real danger that if we wrote off the loan, word would get around that the Bank of Dave was a soft touch. We'd be inundated with loan applications from chancers trying it on with us. It was a difficult situation and I didn't know how to resolve it.

In the end, we wrote it off. It was an act of charity. If it was true that this woman had been beaten up and had lost her job, I decided that I couldn't be yet another source of stress and misery in her life. What was more, I couldn't get away from the fact that her not paying was as much my fault as hers. I'd made a bad call. My judgement had been wrong. Perhaps I'd been wearing rose-tinted glasses, and in my eagerness to help had been too profligate with the bank's money. It was a lesson learned early, and writing off this loan was to be the exception, not the rule. Just as David H had predicted, I would have to be more cautious when it came to unsecured personal loans. If there was even the shadow of a suspicion in our minds that someone was going to blow the money on a holiday in Magaluf and then be unable to pay back the loan, I mustn't go near them. At the end of my 180 days, I would be giving whatever profits the bank made to worthwhile causes. The Joe Bloggs' Magaluf Holiday Fund was not a worthwhile cause.

Naively or not, however, I liked to think that the community and philanthropic nature of my enterprise meant that individual borrowers would be more likely to pay back their personal loans than they would if we were just some faceless corporation trying to line our own pockets with their interest. Failing to pay us back was not the same as failing to pay back a loan shark. There would be very real consequences far beyond the question of whether some rich bastard gets a bit richer. And although there's no doubt that after our fingers were initially burned we became increasingly wary of lending money on this riskier basis, we still said 'yes' to plenty of people who had received nothing but 'no' elsewhere. And as I write these words, the overwhelming majority of these individuals have been good for the money. It's amazing what a little bit of mutual trust can achieve.

And it's also amazing the difference a tiny sum of money can make to some people – from the fella who needed a few quid to make sure Santa was able to visit his little boy Charlie and his brothers and sisters at Christmas, to a little old lady whose car had broken down. The engine needed replacing and she simply didn't have the spare cash to pay for it. Which was a problem, because her husband was in hospital, and she relied on that car to go and visit him every day. Of course, it would be no skin off the rosy noses of the big banks if this elderly couple were unable to be together. But I defy anyone looking at them as real people rather than information on a computer screen, not to want to give them a helping hand if it's possibly within their power to do so.

THE BATTLE OF BURNLEY

The Bank of Dave had barely been open for three months. Already we were lending out something of the order of £25,000 a week. That money was going directly to local businesses and individuals who were struggling to get credit elsewhere.

The interest that they were – with only a few exceptions – paying was being used partly to lend out again and partly to pay a much higher interest rate on deposits than anyone could get elsewhere on the high street. It was beginning to look as if there really was a better way to do banking, if only we could find a way to take deposits.

Banks, however, do more than just savings and loans. If I wanted to compare myself with them, like for like, I wanted to do everything the big boys did. That meant diversification. Or in other words, not putting all my eggs in one basket.

All banks diversify. They don't just rely on their loans to provide them with profit; they invest their money in other ways, like property, commodities and equities. Don't worry if these words are waffle. They are to lots of people. But like most things in banking, they are actually a lot simpler than the bankers would like you to believe. At least, they should be.

The reason it's good to diversify is that it allows you to avoid putting yourself in a situation where your entire pot is at risk from losing money because the bottom falls out of an entire sector. For example, if you've invested everything in property, and there's a property crash, that's a big chunk of all your money lost. But if you've invested half your money in Coca-Cola shares, it's hopefully protected from the housing market crash, and might even go up.

If the Bank of Dave was to do everything that an ordinary bank does, I wanted to invest in property. I knew for a fact that all the big banks had property on their asset sheets. Sometimes, of course, they end up with properties they don't really want on account of people defaulting on loans against which the properties have been put up as security. But, in the past, they've also gone out there specifically to buy properties as investments. Generally, they're large investments – entire car dealerships, for example. Knowing what we now do about the banks, it probably wouldn't surprise us to learn that these investments are not always of the highest quality. Bearing in mind the Bank of Dave's mantra was that we couldn't be bigger than the others, but we could be better, I decided to apply my own ethos to property investment. Being a tiny bank, I couldn't go out and buy a branch of Tesco to back up my savers' money. Moreover, I had to stick to what I knew about. And what *do*

I know about? Buying, selling and renting tiny houses in the residential areas of Burnley.

I've been buying houses in Burnley and Nelson ever since I started out. Whenever I had a bit of spare cash, I wouldn't spend it – never spend your stake, remember – but would buy a house and rent it out. I've still got the first place I ever bought, and I still rent it out. It has gone up and down in value over the years, just like all of them, but properly managed they've always been good investments, even if they're not the biggest, fanciest loft apartments in the UK's biggest, fanciest cities. And the people I rent my places out to aren't the crème de la crème. They're just regular Burnley men and women who need a decent place to live at an affordable rate. When you're renting property, as soon as you start being greedy you're on a losing streak. It's much better to charge a reasonable rent and have a place occupied, than to have an expensive but empty house. And during my years in the property game, I've seen it all.

I have one property that cost me £14,000 many years ago, and which I've been renting out ever since. Eight or nine years back, I took on a tenant. I didn't know it at the time, but he was very heavily into war films and all things military. And unbeknown to me, he bought himself a First World War explosive device off some bloke on the internet. When the device arrived, he wanted to see how it was put together, so he got himself a screwdriver and a hammer and started whacking the back of it with everything he had. It exploded (it was, after all, an explosive device), and sent him through the front of the house. The police thought he was a terrorist; the whole street got evacuated; the house itself was thigh deep in rubble. My tenant was lucky to be alive – he now has a big steel plate in his chest.

But he loved his war, did this fella. He loved the fact that there was blood on the walls as a result of his own little Battle of Burnley – so much so that he kept it up there for months afterwards.

I fixed the house up for him and let him move back in. A mistake? Probably, because the next thing I knew, he'd burned the back of the house down by leaving a chip pan on the stove. And do you want to know the really scary thing? He was, by a country mile, my best tenant. He was in the longest, and he always paid his rent, every month, on the nose.

My point is this: I *know* about renting property in Burnley and Nelson. I know the pitfalls and the problems. I know which end of which street is good, and which is bad. If I plough Burnley Savings and Loans' money in a property into my local town, it's not just a random investment. It's got a bit of know-how behind it. Why anyone would try to invest money in something they don't understand is a mystery to me.

The first house bought in the name of Burnley Savings and Loans is a tiny terraced house in a backstreet of the town. Perhaps, to look at it, you might think it's not much of an investment. It's not in the most desirable part of the country; it's not even in the most desirable part of Burnley. But sometimes, you've got to look past the obvious. As I was searching for property to buy, it was common knowledge that a new supermarket was going to be built at the end of the road on which this house is situated. You can't have a new supermarket without people to work in it; and people working in the supermarket were going to need somewhere affordable to live nearby. So it struck me that this would be a very rentable property.

The house in question cost me £22,500. Admittedly, it was in a rough state of repair. The bathroom was in the kitchen, for a start. Not *next to* the kitchen; *in* the kitchen. But I knew that with a bit of updating I could make it look top dollar. I budgeted around £7,500 for the update, and my plan was then to rent it out for about £85 a week. This would give Burnley Savings and Loans a return on its investment just shy of 15%. What's more, I knew that once renovated, the house would be worth about £50,000 – already a profit of £20,000 – and it would, over time, continue to increase in value. All in all, we were probably looking at an appreciating asset of about 20%. Good for the bank, and good for Burnley too. There are lots of advantages to putting my money into property in the area. I'll be turning round a local place that would otherwise have become dilapidated; my savers' money will not only be safely invested for them, but also doing some good in the community, giving a local person a good quality home; and because the house is right there, near where I live and on my route into work, I could keep my eye on it – unlike the big banks who plunge their money into assets their personnel will never even *see*. And because I've paid the right price for the house in the first place, I know I'm not going to wake up one morning to find the bank's investment has dropped by 90%. It's not like a stock or a share. No matter what happens, I'll be able to turn up and touch the bank's asset. It'll always be made of stone, it will always be something tangible. After all, if I can have a tenant that blows up the front of a house and burns down the back, and that house can not only be still standing, but earning me an income, there's got to be something inherently solid about it. The Bank of Dave's investment property has been there for the last hundred years, and it'll be there for another hundred years. We've seen how the current economic situation came about in part because the banks lent too much money against houses that weren't worth that amount. Residential property was, in many ways, their downfall. My hope was that, done properly, it could be one of the Bank of Dave's greatest strengths.

There's no shortage of property like the house I bought in Burnley: small, perfectly good, inexpensive places that risk falling into a state of disrepair. And not just in Burnley either. I've no doubt that in towns all across the country there are similar properties that could be bought, done up and rented out at a reasonable rate by enterprising banks who wanted to get a good return on their investments and do a bit of good in the community. Would that really be too much to hope for?

If you cast your mind back to The Boring Bit, you'll remember that we imagined a bank that didn't look after people's money, but after their gold. Our imaginary banker invented paper money as a kind of IOU for the gold he had in his safe. If anybody wanted to withdraw their gold, that was fine (so long as not *everybody* turned up together). In the meantime, the money the bank had issued was backed up by the gold in its safe.

Banks still have gold reserves today, though since the major economies of the world left what was known as the 'gold standard' they don't use it to back up their paper money. Take a tenner down to your local bank and they're not obliged to give you a tenner's worth of gold bullion. But the gold does still have value. A very great value. As I write these words, the price of gold is just over £1,000 per ounce. Why is it so valuable? For the same reason it always was: it's pretty, and rare. (It's estimated that all the gold ever mined would fit in a cube with sides of just over 20 metres.) And you only have to look at the cost of a few diamond rings in the window of your local jeweller to realise the price we place on objects that are pretty and rare.

You're probably aware that swanky City investors buy and sell gold. And as with everything else they buy and sell, they never really see the commodities they're trading. Nobody's swapping actual ingots down the Stock Exchange. As with everything else in the world of banking, the bankers' gold is just numbers on a computer screen. The closest they get to it is when they use their bonuses to buy the missus a necklace at Tiffany for Christmas. But if the big banks had gold in their vaults, and if the bankers made money from trading it, then the Bank of Dave needed to get in on the act. If I was going to sink some of my depositors' money into gold, however, I wanted to do it according to the ethos of the enterprise. I didn't want the bank's gold to be figures on a balance sheet; I wanted it to be real gold, in the safe, something tangible I could see and touch. A tiny gold reserve for a tiny bank. And to help me do this, I wanted somebody who really understood the business of gold. Not a slick, suited commodities trader, but someone immersed in the day-to-day buying and selling of the stuff.

Enter Big Roy.

You remember Big Roy? Burnley's jeweller-in-chief had his shop just a few doors down from the premises in Keirby Walk, and he became rather more than a customer of the Bank of Dave. He was also instrumental in helping me build up the bank's own gold deposits – on a tiny scale, of course. At the end of each day, Roy collects all the scraps of gold that have come his way. And at the end of each day, I buy them off him for the going rate of that weight of gold, and pop them in the safe. There's something rather poignant about seeing these wedding rings and lockets, the love hearts and the eternity bracelets. You can't help wondering who they once belonged to, what sort of sentimental value they had and why they had to be sold. My little bag of gold is like a little bag of memories; follow the stories of each of those items back through time and you would have a history of Burnley like no other. It's also a reminder that in times of economic hardship, it's seldom the rich who suffer. It's not the bankers who are selling their wives' diamond necklaces; it's the man and woman in the street, cashing in small objects of great personal value if not massive financial value, just so that they can pay the bills.

When I had enough gold – approximately £14,000 worth – I decided to have it melted down and turned into a gold bullion bar. A tiny gold bar, but a gold bar nevertheless. With this in mind, Roy and I travelled down to the jewellery quarter in Birmingham – a fascinating part of the city full of jewellery shops and a magnet for bullion dealers. We were here to meet Trevor, a Brummie through and through, who also happened to be an expert gold smelter. He'd been doing it for decades, and he was so sick of seeing gold that he refused to wear a wedding ring. He took my Bag for Life full of golden trinkets and shovelled them into his smelting pot. The gold started to ooze and melt but then, to my surprise, it caught fire. What was happening? Was that my gold gone?

'It's not the gold that's on fire,' Trevor told me. It was the perfume, the aftershave, the dead skin, the years of accumulated grease and dirt – all of it burning away. I stood there watching the remnants of people's lives going up in flames and smoke as the molten gold grew purer and purer. Eventually, Trevor poured it into a mould and turned out the Bank of Dave's gold bullion bar. It didn't look quite as I expected. About the size of a TV remote, but thinner and a good deal heavier, it was rather rough and covered with black stains that Trevor said would only come off with sulphuric acid. It was certainly not one of those great, shiny ingots you see in the movies. But it was beautiful in its own way – more for what it symbolised than how it looked. It would sit in my little safe in my little vault, its value changing with the global gold market, but representing, I hoped, a solid and safe investment for my depositors. And it was pleasing to think that, although those golden trinkets had been sold by people who, if times had been different, might have held on to them and passed them to their children and grandchildren, they would at least now be playing some part in reviving the economic health of the local community. Maybe their children and grandchildren would benefit after all.

It almost goes without saying that I would never have bought property on behalf of the Bank of Dave without looking at it first. And I wouldn't have bought gold off Roy without checking it was the correct carat and the correct price for the correct weight. You wouldn't buy a car without at least a cursory glance at it, would you? And it's always sensible to open up a box of eggs to make sure none of them are cracked. You don't need me to tell you this. It's common sense. Unfortunately, I can think of a place where common sense is in short supply. Can you guess where it is yet?

Back in the day, when I was buying and selling cars, there was a thing called a chucky book – a list of all the loans you'd given on vehicles. If you'd sold a car on finance, each loan you'd made had a certain value, because someone would be paying you interest on that loan. One person's debt is another person's asset. It wasn't uncommon for dealers to buy or sell the chucky book, so that in return for a fee, someone else took over the benefit of the income from those loans. Selling the chucky book isn't limited to the car industry. It happens millions of times, all over the world, every day. Banks do it too, only they've come up with fancier names for the process. Doesn't matter what you call it, though. It's selling the chucky book through and through.

We know that the recent economic crisis was triggered by toxic loans in the US housing market. Lenders had lent too much money against properties that weren't worth that amount to individuals who weren't in a position to repay those sums. You haven't got to be Brain of Britain to see that it was a financial disaster waiting to happen. The world of banking being what it is, however, the original lenders didn't hold on to these loans for long. They were packaged up into 'parcels' of debt and sold to other banks. And sold again. And insured. And re-insured. They became the basis of complicated financial instruments that nobody really understood. They infected the whole banking system like a cancer. And when the loans went bad, the patient kicked the bucket. The trouble was that nobody had looked too closely at the debt they were buying. If they had, they might have realised it was rotten.

Perhaps you're wondering why anybody would want to sell their debts in the first place. Surely it's not too cynical to think that there might be something *wrong* with the debt? Not always. A company might sell off some of their debt because they're struggling and need to get a bit of cash in their hand; or maybe they need liquidity to expand. There are plenty of reasons for, and nothing inherently wrong, with selling the chucky book, or indeed with buying it. It strikes me that you just have to know what you're buying and reject anything you think might go bad, which would have the knock-on effect of stopping the original lenders from lending irresponsibly in the first place.

Knowing that big banks were in the business of buying and selling parcels of debt, I decided I needed to give it a punt myself. I wouldn't be buying billions of pounds' worth of dodgy mortgages, of course. Tiny bank, tiny parcel of debt. But it didn't matter to me how big or small it was. What mattered was that I *knew* what I was buying.

I found a little finance firm that was looking to sell off some of its vehicle loans and personal loans. The details of these individual debts came in a large envelope, but before I agreed to spend a penny of Burnley Savings and Loans' money, I did what the banks failed to do before the crisis: I opened up the envelope and I looked inside. I examined each and every debt in that parcel, and I made an individual judgement on each one. I found out who had borrowed the money, and if it was a vehicle loan what car they'd borrowed it against, was the car worth more than the balance of the loan? In short, would I have lent any of the bank's money to the borrower in question in the first place? I had to be careful. The parcel of loans wasn't cheap. The sums involved might have been peanuts to one of the big banks; but they could have finished the Bank of Dave in an instant if they'd gone bad. Anything I didn't like the look of, I put to one side.

If I didn't like it, I wasn't buying it. The big banks might have been happy to play fast and loose with their borrowers' money; I wasn't.

I don't think I was being unduly cautious. Quite the opposite. I don't care if we're talking about a hundred quid personal loan or a hundred million quid commercial loan. It's stunningly obvious that the banks should have done exactly the same thing. They should have opened up the envelope, and checked what was inside.

It might be, of course, that they *did* open up the envelope, take a peek and quickly flog it on to the next person when they saw what they'd bought. In that case, I can't help thinking they deserve everything they got. It's just a shame everybody else had to suffer on account of it.

Savings and loans. Property investment. Commodities. Parcels of debt. I was beginning to feel that, in its tiny way, the Bank of Dave really was doing the things a big bank does. Were we doing it better? I think so. We were investing wisely in areas we knew something about. We weren't immune to risk; but we weren't being daft with other people's money. No doubt there'd be plenty of people in the City who thought our operation was tinpot and homespun. But it was working, which was more than could be said about many of their financial institutions. And already, the positive effects of the enterprise were being felt in the local community.

That didn't mean, however, that it was a success. I still had no banking licence. I still could not take deposits from anybody other than high-net-worth individuals. I still couldn't take Betty's money. And that meant that my 5% savings rate was having only one effect: the rich were getting richer, and that had never been the plan.

And something else was missing too. Something that all banks did, and which had the potential to make – and lose – a fortune. It was this activity that created some of the biggest baddies of the banking crisis, the speculators and hedge-fund managers whose pockets were lined with gold while everyone else was suffering. I wanted to demonstrate what they did and how they did it. I wanted to show them up. I wanted to take them on, and win.

There's no Stock Exchange in Burnley. That's why, halfway through my 180 days I got myself on a plane from Manchester and flew to New York. My destination was Wall Street. It was time for the Bank of Dave to go global.

PART 3

GREED ISN'T GOOD

Picture it: you've had a hard day at work, you've eaten your tea, you've watched *Corrie*, you've had a brew. It's time for bed. You're probably not thinking too much about the contents of your bank account, about what's happening to your hard-earned money while you sleep. Perhaps you should.

We've already seen that the traditional banking model is based on a little sleight of hand. We all assume that if our bank balance says £200, that money's actually in the bank. It isn't. Some of it has (or should have been) loaned out. Our ability to withdraw our £200 relies on the assumption that not everybody will try to withdraw all their money at the same time. But what about the money we deposit with our banks that *doesn't* get lent out? Does it just sit in their coffers, gathering dust, while we sleep? Hardly. Enter the murky world of investment banking: a world where, through dealing in stocks and shares, fortunes can be won, and lost, in seconds.

At the time of the financial crisis, all the major high street banks had investment arms. And the big names that you heard being bandied around – Lehman Brothers, Bear Stearns,

Goldman Sachs – are, or were, investment banks. Broadly speaking, investment banks do two things. Firstly, they advise big firms on strategies for raising money. Secondly, they deal in the financial markets for their own profit, and it's this that has had a direct effect on you and me.

Investing money ought to be very simple. You buy a share in a company you think will be profitable in the future. You hope that share price will go up. You buy low, you sell high. The bit in the middle is yours. And as with most aspects of banking, there doesn't seem to me to be much wrong with it, so long as it's done right. If you've done your homework on a company, if you like and understand their product or their service, if you think it's well run and has potential, why the hell shouldn't you invest a few quid in their fortunes? That's not to say that there isn't a risk. Of course there is. If the share price goes down, under ordinary circumstances you'll lose money. I say 'under ordinary circumstances' because, as per usual, the bankers have taken something that should be simple and made it a great deal more complicated. But we'll get to that.

I wanted Burnley Savings and Loans to do everything the big banks do. I didn't have billions to invest on the global financial markets, but I did want the money we had on deposit to work hard. I had, after all, promised to pay 5% interest, and you don't do that by letting piles of cash sit in the safe gathering dust. But there was more to my desire to invest in the markets than keeping up with the Joneses. The Bank of Dave had a point to prove.

As I write this, the rate of interest you or I would get from one of the big banks is in the region of 0.1% to 0.25%. Think about that. If you give Barry the Banker a hundred quid, and let him keep it for a year, at the end of that year he'll give you a maximum of 25 pence in interest. If he takes that hundred quid, invests it in the stock market and, at the end of the year, makes more than 25 pence profit, he's in the money. If he invests the hundred quid sensibly, he'll probably make a lot more than 25 pence profit. If he invests it recklessly, there's a chance that he'll make an enormous profit, but there's also a chance that he'll lose the lot. The lower the risk, the lower the potential returns. The higher the risk, the higher the potential returns. You pay your money, you take your chance.

Your average trader – let's call him Terry – is paid a great deal to make these decisions. Terry the Trader will tell you he's worth every penny. Speculating on the stock market is a highly skilled profession. Only the elite few can understand it in any depth. Even when he gets it wrong, he'll tell you, and his bank has to be bailed out with our money, it remains very important to pay him handsomely. If we don't, Terry would be forced to take his skills elsewhere, and what kind of a mess would we be in then?

But just imagine this. What if a lad from Burnley with no qualifications and no experience of investment banking spent one day investing in the markets, and managed to make more profit in one day than the banks pay in interest in a year? What if he did this while the banks in the UK were all shut up for the night, pretending that their depositors' money was safe and sound, when in fact Terry the Trader is using it to gamble on international markets all round the world? Would that be possible? And if it was, what would it say about these banks that have lost billions of dollars?

This was the task I set myself. I didn't just want the Bank of Dave to be better than the banks on the high street. I wanted it to be better than those on Wall Street too.

Wall Street, Manhattan, is the centre of the global financial system. The hub. The engine room. The Bank of Dave might only have been a tiny operation from Burnley, Lancashire, but Wall Street was where I wanted to be. I would go there, I decided, with the equivalent of $100,000 of Burnley Savings and Loans's money. While the banks in the UK were shut, I'd spend a day playing the markets. If I could make between 2% and 3% in one day, and the banks are only giving you .25% for a year, then they've got some serious explaining to do.

I'll come clean. I'm not entirely inexperienced in the business of buying and selling stocks and shares. I'm by no means a pro, but I've had a bit of a go at it. But I'm not one of these traders with their fancy computer systems and complicated financial instruments, and I don't really think you have to be. Investing on the stock market isn't rocket science, even though there are plenty of people out there who will try to tell you it is, and I'll let you into a little secret: my approach to buying and selling stocks and shares on the New York Stock Exchange isn't very different to the approach I adopted in deciding which businesses to lend the Bank of Dave's money to in Burnley. It's a secret I'm happy to share with anybody who wants to listen.

Anyone who wants to invest on the stock market needs to educate themselves. I don't mean that you have to go off to business school or weigh yourself down with qualifications. You don't have to be of professor of Difficult Maths to work out all those graphs and figures. But you *do* have to understand what you're doing. Ask questions. Read up. There's no shortage of advice out there, on the financial pages of the newspapers, on the internet or from brokers whose job it is to monitor the stock market on a daily basis and to be hugely well informed and full of good suggestions. Read and listen to this advice by all means, but do your own research too. Believe in yourself. No matter what advice I've received in the past, I wouldn't think of investing a single pound of my money in a company I knew nothing about, no matter how many people told me it was a great idea. And that's the point. In the world of stocks and shares, everyone has an opinion. You'll find one person betting massive sums that a stock will go up, you'll find another person betting massive sums that it'll go down. Educate yourself, but remember: the only person whose opinion matters is your own. If you don't have a well-informed opinion on a particular company, how can you make a sensible decision whether or not to invest in it?

This might sound bloody obvious, but you'd be surprised. There are plenty of traders, hedge funds and whoever, who play around with what's known as 'black-box trading'. Instead of having someone making judgements about the strength of a company, they let a computer do it. The 'black box' crunches numbers and buys and sells shares on the back of its algorithms. There's no relationship between an investor and the company it's investing in. Quite how these traders justify fat bonuses when a computer has done all the work is beyond me, but remember this: every day about seven billion shares are traded in America, and about 70% of them are traded by black boxes.

So what makes a good company? How do you form an opinion? I've already talked about Coca-Cola and in *my* opinion it's hard to think of a safer, better-run firm. Its brand is recognised the world over, and although people have tried to go after its business many times in the past, they have always failed. The firm is as close to untouchable as it's possible to be. Everyone understands the product – show me someone who's never had a can of Coke – which means the man in the street can make a sensible judgement about it. Does Coca-Cola stock go down as well as up? Of course it does. But I can't stress enough that investing is for the long term. If you fly into a panic every time the value of one of your investments dips slightly, you're missing the point. You should be backing the long-term prospects of the company, not trying to make a cheeky quick buck on its short-term fluctuations. Don't believe me? Then listen to one of my heroes, Warren Buffett. My investment strategy is his investment strategy, and it hasn't done him any harm – sensible investments in solid companies that appreciate slowly but reliably over time. Probably sounds a bit boring, right? But I know that if *I* had a few quid stashed away in my bank account, that's how I'd want it to be invested. Remember Betty? Remember how she invested her life savings on the advice of one of the big banks, only to lose a huge chunk of it? I wouldn't stand for that happening with the Bank of Dave – not least because I was guaranteeing everybody's money personally.

You'd think, wouldn't you, that traders in the big investment banks would have a similar strategy. Many of them do. But some don't. Share prices can fluctuate massively, not only over a period of days, but over hours and even minutes. Buy a stock at 100 pence at 10am, and sell it for 150 pence at 11am – hey presto, you've made 50% profit in an hour. You can see how people might be tempted. It's the same mentality that makes casinos so popular. If you head to the roulette wheels of Las Vegas and put all your money on black, you have a fairly good chance of doubling it. (In Vegas, of course, you have a fractionally bigger chance of losing it all too. The casinos are very careful to make sure that the odds are always slightly stacked in their favour.) In many ways, speculating on the stock market is the same as gambling in Vegas. Get it right and you win, get it wrong and you lose. They both attract people who get a thrill from the idea of making a fast buck. In a casino you can move from the roulette wheel to the poker table to the slots. There are lots of different games you can play on the markets too. The difference is this: Terry the Trader and all his mates have spent a long time trying to work out ways of stacking the odds in their favour. When they win, they win big and pay themselves eye-watering bonuses. When they lose, they lose big – but, as we've all seen, they get bailed out by the government, and *still* pay themselves eye-watering bonuses. Quite how that works remains a mystery to me. If one of my employees lost a load of money and wanted a bonus, I'd soon tell him where to get off.

I have a friend on Wall Street. His name is Mark Mansour and he works for a brokerage company called PHD Capital. He's a very clever man, speaks several languages and knows the markets like the back of his hand. When I arrived in New York he took me on a tour of the town – not the usual tourist trail of the Empire State Building and the Statue of Liberty, but a trip round the banks and financial institutions that were at the heart of the crisis. They were big, shiny, impressive skyscrapers. But, as I'd learned through my experiences with the Bank of Dave, size isn't everything. It's not what you've got that's important – it's what you do with it.

We also discussed in detail the stocks and shares that I should buy on the big day. And, in my mind, it *was* a big day. I was nervous – more nervous than I'd been at any point during my whole Bank of Dave journey. I had come to Wall Street with a point to prove, namely that it was possible to invest sensibly and still make a higher percentage profit in a day than the banks were paying in interest in a year. More than ever, it was me against them. I was putting my money where my mouth was. Any losses Burnley Savings and Loans suffered, I would cough up from my own resources, so there was no risk to my depositors' money. But as you probably know by now, I was far more concerned about losing face than I was about losing money. The trouble was, even the safest stock can go down over a single trading day, and I wasn't using black boxes or clever algorithms. I was just using a bit of northern nous.

PHD Capital is run by two guys with a massive amount of experience, Nelson Braff and Jody Eisenman. Nelson is the part-owner with Justin Timberlake of a New York restaurant. The evening before the day of the trade, Mark took me to dinner there, and we spent some time with Nelson discussing what my strategy should be for the following day. I'd like to think I listened to everything they said with an open mind. Nelson and Mark are experts in their field and there was no way I was going to be so arrogant as to ignore their advice and their guidance. I would take on board everything they had to say, I decided, but when the chips were down, the decision about where to invest the bank's money would be mine, and mine alone. And as I sat in the restaurant, listening to Nelson and Mark talking, it was brought home to me that, although these guys really were top dogs when it came to playing the markets, they could only *speculate* about what was going to happen the following day. Nobody knows for sure whether a given stock is going to rise or fall. The best you can do is make an informed guess. There really is very little between investing on the stock market and gambling, or between a seasoned pro and a well-informed amateur.

The following day, Mark took me to his offices on Wall Street where I met his boss Jody. Here was another man with massive amounts of experience – trust me, you don't own a stockbroking firm on Wall Street without knowing your stuff. I would be an idiot if I didn't listen to what he had to say. We sat together in the minutes before the markets opened, and I asked him what he thought I should do.

'Short the market,' he told me – stockbroker-speak for betting that the market is going to go down.

So how does that work? How can you make money on a share that goes down in value? Here's how. You borrow a stock from someone who already owns it. You then sell it at the market price. If the value of the stock *does* go down, you can buy it back at the cheaper price before returning it to its owner. You sell high, and buy low. The bit in the middle is yours. The question of whether short selling is good or bad for the economy is not one for this book, but one thing is sure: it *is* risky. If I buy a stock for $100 in the hope that it will go up in price, the worst thing that can happen is that its value reduces to zero and I've lost $100. If I short a stock for $100 in the hope it will go *down* to $50, there's no limit to how *high* it could go. The higher it goes, the more I lose. The losses can be massive.

So shorting is risky, but it's the way to make money if you think the market is going to fall, so maybe I needed to think about it. I listened to what Jody had to say, and I listened carefully. This was a man who had spent his whole professional life working in the financial markets. He and his people made a *lot* of money doing it. But there was a problem: I just wasn't convinced by what I heard. It wasn't just that shorting the market didn't feel like the kind of thing the Bank of Dave should be doing – I wanted to encourage businesses, not bet on their failure – it was also that I didn't have the impression that it was the right move to make.

It was a proper dilemma. I was gambling $100,000 of the Bank of Dave's money. Should I go with my gut instinct? Or should I, for once in my life, put my own opinions to one side and listen to the experts?

I sat with Mark at his desk. In front of us was a computer terminal that would allow us to drop the bank's money on to the New York Stock Exchange and track the trades over the next few hours. And as we waited for the markets to open, I had a simple choice to make: did I go short, like Jody had recommended, or long, in line with everything I'd ever believed about investing in stocks and shares?

I turned to Mark. 'I'm going long,' I said.

I think he thought I was crazy. 'But Jody's going short,' he told me. '*Everyone's* going short.'

I shook my head. 'I want to go long. I'm going to pick some really solid stocks and I'm going to do what I think's right.'

And so, when the markets opened, I dropped $50,000 into Visa stocks, and $12,500 into a company called Walter Energy Inc.

I was confident that Visa was a fantastic stock. Everyone's got one in their pocket, they don't bet their own money, they've got billions in the bank and they make a profit every year. It's not going to go bankrupt, it's got nobody silly running it. It's a solid, well-run company with a moat around it – very difficult for any competitors to come after. Visa is the sort of stock I'd personally be very comfortable owning for ever, so where else would Burnley Savings and Loans' money be better off?

Walter Energy was an aggressively moving stock. I wouldn't want to put all my money into it, but I could see that although there was a small chance of making a loss on it, there was a greater chance of making a profit, and a good one at that.

Buying those stocks was as easy as pressing a button. And as I sat there, waiting to press it, I felt like an old-fashioned sniper with a target in his sights, waiting to discharge his only bullet, knowing that he only had one chance to get it right. Hold it... hold it...*fire!*

I fired.

Within seconds of the markets opening, I'd spent two-thirds of the bank's $100,000. And the moment I dropped the trades, both stocks plummeted.

My stomach sank with them. In an instant, thousands of dollars had been slashed off the Bank of Dave's assets. A voice in my head started giving me a hard time: I should have listened to the experts. I should have gone short.

I stood up, feeling slightly sick. I walked around the office. I tried to get my head clear and to remind myself of everything I believed about investments: that it was their long-term prospects that mattered, not what happened from one minute to the next. I hadn't been a sheep, I'd done what I believed was right. And I reminded myself of a little maxim. When all around are fearful, be greedy. When all around are greedy, be fearful. I sat myself down in front of the screen again, and told myself to get back in the game.

The initial scramble that often happens at the opening of the markets started to subside. As it did, Visa started to creep back up. So did Walter Energy. Gradually I crept back into the green.

Then down into the red again.

Back into the green.

The red.

But although the stocks were fluctuating, they were heading in the right direction. Before long they were firmly in the green.

By the time I'd finished trading, the $50,000 I'd dropped on Visa had made a fraction over 1%. Perhaps that doesn't sound a lot? When you consider, though, that this is profit earned over a period of just three or four hours, it's colossal. As I write this book, if you were to put $50,000 of your own money in a regular savings account, it would take you *four years* to earn that kind of interest. Think about that: little Dave, who sells buses in Burnley, went to Wall Street and made four years' interest in four hours.

You're probably thinking: perhaps it was a fluke? Well perhaps it was. But the money I put on WLT also made just over 1%. So perhaps it *wasn't* a fluke. Perhaps investing safely and sensibly in the stock market is a better strategy than being a flash Harry and getting all greedy with your clever schemes...Of the $100,000 I had set aside to invest that day, I still had $37,000 left. I decided that I would invest this money in a company called RIM. RIM make the BlackBerry. Three years previously they had been trading around the $140 per share mark. Recently they'd been trading between $12 and $17. It seemed to me that the potential up side was massive. The down side? Well, they could go down to under $10. Not the end of the world. They were a company that had more than $1 billion in the bank in reserve just waiting to be invested and they've made a profit every year. That struck me as being a very good, very undervalued, stock. I knew it was never going to rise back up to its historic high, but I also knew there was a very good chance of it going up above $20. And while this wasn't a basket in which I'd put all the bank's eggs, I figured that the potential reward countered the risk.

I wanted to buy some RIM shares, but I wanted to do it a bit differently. I wanted to learn more about the financial weapons of mass destruction that had brought the economy to its knees, but I wanted to see if it was possible to use them in a safe, solid way. I wasn't going risk the bank's money in anything stupidly risky. So I decided to have a go at what is known as 'options' trading. Before your eyes start glazing over, bear with me: you're about to find out just how straightforward it is for Terry the Trader to make money.

An option is the right to buy a stock at some point in the future. So how does that work? Let's imagine that you buy one share in a company for $100. The moment you've bought it, you can sell to another investor the *right* to buy that share at some point in the next 30 days at a given price, *if* they *want* to buy it. So, somebody might pay you $5 for the right to buy that share at some point in the next month for $120. If the stock price goes higher than $120, they'll exercise that option; if it doesn't, they won't. Either way, you've made $5 – that's a 5% return – seconds after you've bought the share. Of course, the share could go down in value, but if you've done your homework, and you're intending to hold on to it for the long term, that shouldn't bother you because you'll be confident that it'll go up again. Whether I sold the option or not, I was happy for Burnley Savings and Loans to hold on to that RIM stock for months and months. I felt confident that it was a good, solid, safe investment for my depositors.

And think about what options trading means from the point of view of the person *buying* the option. They only have to risk $5 to benefit from the stock going up – they don't have to have the $100 to buy it in the first place.

I dropped the remaining $37,500, which was only a small proportion of Burnley Savings and Loans' operating money, on to the New York Stock Exchange. A second – literally a second – afterwards, I sold the options on those shares and made an instant 8% profit. Now, as I'd sold the option, I had to hold on to these shares for thirty days. I knew there was a possibility that they could go down in value over this time. But that didn't worry me, for two reasons. Firstly, I was in it for the long term and I had chosen my stocks carefully. And secondly, even if the share price did go down, I could still sell the option again – and again, and again – and get some kind of return on my investment.

Traders like to pretend that what they do is complicated. They like to pretend that they are worth their massive bonuses because they have a special skill that very few of us ordinary mortals can get our heads round. But here's the thing: if I can keep making 5% or 8% every time I sell an option on a stock, it doesn't take a brain surgeon to work out that we've been duped by these bankers who keep saying that their financial instruments and mathematical equations and all this other stuff they've been going on about is far too difficult for the likes of you and me to understand. If they can do it, anybody can do it.

You'll have your own opinions about whether shorting stocks, options trading and all the other games the banks have invented to make money are a good thing or a bad thing. My intention was just to show that, contrary to what people who deal in the financial markets would like you to believe, it's not rocket science. It's glorified gambling, and while the professionals might understand the rules of the game a bit better than you or me, they can't predict the future, no matter what they tell you.

At the end of my day on Wall Street, when everything was taken into account and the money I'd made on Visa, Walter Energy and selling the options on my RIM stock was totted up, I'd made just under 3.25% profit on the Bank of Dave's money. In one day. My mentors, who had made the decision to go short rather than long, lost money. It didn't mean I was better than Mark, Jody or Nelson. But it did bring home to me that in a world where you're gambling your money, the opinions of experts need to be taken with a pinch of salt.

As I write, there is all sorts of talk about separating the savings and loans side of banking from the investment side. This would mean that the investment banks would not be able to use depositors' money to speculate on the stock market. Is this a good thing? Should I have been allowed to take the Bank of Dave's money and gamble it on Wall Street? I'm in two minds. The truth is, by the time I went to New York, I was already making a profit from the savings and loans side of the business. I was well on my way to proving that it could be done. It was clear to me, though, that the investment side had the potential to make the Bank of Dave a lot more profit, and I had no real problem with that, so long as the investments were solid, safe and careful. Would I be risking millions on highly volatile stocks? Would I be handing my customers' hard-earned cash over to some computer to invest the money on the basis of complicated algorithms and long equations rather than a good, clear understanding of the companies in which they were investing, and the people running them? Would I be paying myself a big fat bonus for all my clever work, and cutting the rate of interest the Bank of Dave was able to pay?

No. Not on your nelly.

I felt like I'd come a long way since that moment back in 2008 when my bank manager sat in my office and tried to lend me money I didn't need instead of entrusting it to local businesses who did. The time, all those months ago, when the world and his wife was telling me that I was mad to try to set up my own tiny bank, that what I wanted to do couldn't be done, seemed a long way in the past. The Bank of Dave was up and running. It was profitable, and it was doing what it had set out to do. It was, I felt sure, a positive influence on the community.

I could actively see things changing. The changes were small, perhaps. A big bank would probably have thought they were insignificant. Shaun the boat builder had erected a second polytunnel so he could have two boats on the go at the same time. Christine and Keith could prepare food for their cafe without worrying whether the tables were going to collapse underneath them. Punters were walking through the doors of Steve's pet shop to see the sharks. After an amazing launch day, where the shop was the busiest it had been for five years, his profits had suddenly increased. Work had started on the shop front of Rachel the florist. Robert the busker could busk. Children who might not otherwise have had Christmas presents had woken up on Christmas morning to see that Santa had been. These small loans were making a big, positive difference to people's lives, and there seemed to be no shortage of people in desperate need of the money.

High Adventure is a residential outdoor education centre for children and young adults. It was founded by four PE teachers – now, unfortunately, only three as they lost one of their number, Lynn, to cancer. Just inside their premises, an ornately carved totem pole has been erected in Lynn's memory. It's a poignant sight, a reminder that businesses are not just about money and profit, but about people. And if ever this was true of any business, it's true of this one. A few miles out of Nelson, High Adventure has a real, positive influence on the lives of all the kids that pass through its doors. There are climbing walls and high wires, abseiling walls and obstacle courses where the students have to learn how to work together and help each other to solve problems. Inside, they have the Labyrinth, a dark, underfloor maze where image-conscious sixteen-year-olds, unseen by their mates, can become kids again like they should be, rather than trying to be adults before their time.

The facilities at High Adventure are brilliant, but the guys who run it don't just keep the kids cooped up on the premises. They also take them out into the countryside where they can try their hand at orienteering and canoeing, and even go caving in the Yorkshire Dales. They employ 25 full-time, permanent staff and lots of trainees. Plenty of kids come to them as students, go on to do work experience and trainee stints, and are now working in the industry themselves.

High Adventure is a good, solid, profitable business. But it's more than that. It's an organisation that makes a difference. Chris, one of the directors, explained to me that he'd seen any number of kids, clearly in danger of going off the rails, whose eyes had been opened by what they could achieve with a little application and teamwork. For my money, that alone is something worth investing in.

The firm's previous bank clearly didn't agree. High Adventure had what is known as an 'offset' commercial mortgage. Any cash that came in paid off the firm's mortgage and decreased its interest payments; if cash flow was tight, it could then increase its mortgage to cover it. It's in the nature of High Adventure's business that its income waxes and wanes a little. Sometimes, if the firm had taken several payments from school parties wanting to use its facilities, it would have a fairly substantial chunk of cash. Using it to pay down its debt worked well. Other times, High Adventure might be waiting on money to come in, in which case it would make use of its mortgage. Obviously the firm was careful, and tried to make sure that, at the time the bank calculated how much interest it owed, its borrowings were low. That's just good business sense.

Unfortunately, the bank decided that this system was working less well for them than it was for High Adventure. Without any warning, the bank withdrew the facility. Why? Chris and his other directors didn't know. They could only assume that the bank simply wasn't making enough money out of High Adventure. There certainly appeared to be no thought for the positive things the business was doing in the community, or what effect the bank's decision might have on the people involved. Just a letter in the post: sorry, mate, we've changed our mind. Instead, the bank offered the firm a loan, but naturally this was a lot more favourable to the bank than it was to High Adventure. Oh, and they wanted a £2,000 'arrangement fee' to set it up.

This bombshell came at exactly the wrong time. High Adventure was relying on the drawdown facility of its mortgage to pay for an extension which was being built. The firm had already booked the builder – a local trader who had put aside three months to do the work. Knowing that if they pulled out now, it would have a dreadful effect on the builder's own business, Chris and his other directors remained committed to the extension. (If only everyone had that kind of integrity.) Now, however, High Adventure had to pay for it out of cash flow, which hit the firm hard. The directors stopped paying themselves so they could carry on paying their staff. Through no fault of their own, and out of a desire just to do the right thing, their good little business was looking threatened.

Every business has expenses – items it *needs* to keep the show on the road. High Adventure is no different. Just like a busker needs an amp, High Adventure needs a fleet of minibuses. These vehicles are an essential tool of its trade. Without the buses, it would have no means of getting the kids out into the Dales and the surrounding countryside. But at a time when the firm was getting so little support from the banks, cash flow was tight and its old fleet of well-used vehicles was coming to the end of its life, High Adventure needed someone to give it a helping hand – someone who wouldn't turn down the company simply because it wasn't making enough money out of them. Enter the Bank of Dave. I could see that the cost of replacing a fleet of minibuses would simply be an impossible expense for High Adventure. But I could also see that these were decent, honest, ethical people with a sound business, prepared to move hell or high water to honour their commitments and keep their business afloat. I was happy to lend them the money at a reasonable rate to enable them to do so. They were able to replace the firm's fleet so that it could safely and reliably ferry the students around, and it also used part of the loan to replace some of its canoes. It almost goes without saying that, as I write this, High Adventure has been as regular with their repayments as I knew it would be. And I don't know about you, but I think that the way a good business like this has been treated by its bank is a scandal. High Adventure has done nothing wrong and everything right. It is not just helping the economy to grow. It is helping *people* to grow. We should be fighting to keep businesses like this going, not looking for every opportunity to shaft them.

I was very proud of what my tiny bank was doing in terms of giving a little bit of help to struggling local businesses who needed it. But there was still a problem: I had no banking licence, and no realistic prospect of getting one.

The authorities still didn't appear to share my vision for a bank that wasn't there just to make the bankers richer. As a result, I could still only take deposits from high net-worth individuals. Even though I knew there were ordinary folk queuing up to earn 5% interest on their savings instead of the paltry .25% the big banks were offering them, I just couldn't take their money. If I did, I could go to prison. It was all back to front. I didn't start this bank to make rich people richer; but I could take money from the wealthy all day long, turn it into more money, and nobody would bat an eyelid. But could I give the savers who most needed it a bit of a helping hand? Could I take money from Betty, the woman who'd had such a raw deal from the big banks? 'Fraid not. It looked like the banking system was set up to help the rich and not the poor. I was being shafted by the R word: regulation.

On the face of it, regulation doesn't seem to be such a bad thing. There are very good reasons for not allowing any old Johnny-come-lately to encourage members of the public to give him their money. We only have to look at the likes of Bernie Madoff to realise that the world of finance is a magnet for crooks willing to fill their boots by ripping people off. I remembered Giles from Zopa telling me that he longed for the FSA to regulate them, presumably because the FSA stamp of approval would make people think better of the firm and bring more business their way. But the way I saw it, regulation hadn't stopped the big boys from losing Betty's money. It hadn't stopped the banks totally messing things up. It hadn't stopped them from losing billions of pounds of our money. So was it really everything it was cracked up to be?

As you know, I started out in life buying and selling cars. It's a business that has a bit of a reputation as being full of scallywags and conmen. Unlike the world of banking, it's entirely unregulated, and lots of people think it's a magnet for Arthur Daleys as a result. But I can assure you of this: there's more honour in the world of used-car salesmen than there is in the whole of the banking industry. It's true that you don't have to fill in an 8,000-page application form to sell cars. It's true that you don't have to put up millions of quids in security. It's true that anyone can do it. But the fact that it isn't regulated *doesn't* mean it's full of dodgy geezers. Back in the day, if I had a car and you offered me a thousand quid for it, and we shook on the deal, there was no way I would even *think* about going back on our agreement. Even if you hadn't paid me, if someone came in and offered me twice as much money, I would have put the two of you in touch so that you could do your own deal with him. Can you imagine something similar happening in the banking industry? Not a bloody chance. Everyone's out for what they can get – they'll do it by any legal means possible and bollocks to the ethics of the situation. And the reason for that is that the banks are regulated to buggery. As a result, they're *allowed* to lose your money. It's legalised ripping off, no two ways about it, and if that's regulation then as far as I'm concerned the authorities can shove it where the sun doesn't shine.

Banking regulations have grown with the industry, which is why they're so unwieldy and complicated. But the Bank of Dave was getting back to basics: if you give me a pound, I promise to give it you back, plus 5 pence extra, at the end of a year. We don't need a piece of paper to remember what we're doing here, let alone thousands of pages of regulations. The way I saw it, there would only be a problem with not being regulated if I did something wrong – if I ripped off someone, or stole their money, or lost it (like the big boys did with Betty). But the whole point of my endeavour was that that wasn't going to happen. If something *did* go wrong, I'd be putting my hand in my pocket to make it right again.

Given that I was personally guaranteeing everybody's money, I don't think you needed to be a brain surgeon to realise that depositors were getting a much better deal with the Bank of Dave than they were with any of the big boys. I'd learned, however, that common sense doesn't hold much sway with the banking authorities, and that if I thought I was going to get a deposit-taking licence before my 180 days were up, I was in cloud cuckoo land, just like everybody had told me right at the beginning.

Although I'd been a success in terms of doing everything else that a big bank does, I knew that if I didn't solve the problem of taking Betty's money, the whole project would, in my eyes, have been a failure. Me being me, that wasn't something I was prepared to let happen. To hell with the FSA and their stupid rules. I was going to find a way to take a pound off an old lady if it was the last thing I did.

You remember the Bolt, right? This was my way of getting round the authorities' refusal to meet with me to discuss getting a banking licence without having to pay millions or wait years. Two components were fully in place: I could lend money, and I could take deposits from other businesses and high net-worth individuals. Because I had no banking licence, I wanted to bolster the third component: my personal guarantee that I would pay back all of my customers' money, plus interest, no matter what. Being unregulated, I couldn't take advantage of the Financial Services Compensation Scheme guaranteeing depositors' money up to the sum of £85,000 per person per institution. But so what? I wanted to do better than that. I wanted to cover every penny of every person's money that came into the Bank of Dave. I decided to look into getting an insurance policy. That way, I could show people I was putting my money where my mouth was.

I approached a major insurance company to see if they would give me a catch-all insurance for everything I needed.

They didn't want to know – I think they thought I was bonkers. Back to square one: there *had* to be a way round it. First off, I got myself some life insurance. If I dropped dead, my depositors' money needed to be covered. Secondly, I arranged a fidelity insurance, which is a policy designed to pay out if I run off to the Bahamas with all the money. Thirdly, I arranged a personal guarantee, backed up by property that I own, in case everything goes bad. Burnley Savings and Loans has first dibs on those properties if it starts to lose money. These three components form a single certificate, for which the bank is charged a monthly fee. As the deposits grow, so does the fee, and it means that the Bank of Dave is probably the safest place in the world anybody could put their money. But even with this insurance in place, your average granny wanting to get a decent rate of interest on her nest egg couldn't entrust me with a single penny. It was illegal. I'd go to prison. So what was I to do?

There was still the possibility of forming a credit union, but predictably enough the more I looked into it, the more layers of bullshit there were to wade through. And the bottom line was that I didn't really *want* to be a credit union. It would have been too restrictive. I'd only have been able to lend out a certain proportion of what I had in the bank; I'd only have been able to lend to people who lived in a certain area. It transpired that the bank would have had to pay £4,000 in training fees before I could even *apply* for the bloody thing. Once again, I felt like people were chucking obstacles in my path. I wanted to do something very simple. They wanted to make it very complicated. I had to keep the credit union in mind, but it would have been a third-rate fall-back position. And the clock was ticking. My 180 days were almost up. It was beginning to look as if it was that, or nothing.

Until finally, just a couple of weeks before my deadline, we had a breakthrough.

Remember Giles from Zopa? He had predicted, all those months ago, that at some stage I would have to consider going down the same line as him: the line of what is known as 'peer to peer lending'. Zopa's business model was this: they matched people wanting to borrow money with people wanting to invest it, and they charged a fee for the service. It wasn't what I wanted to do – not by a long shot – but it gave me and my solicitors an idea. And it was from this seed of an idea that the solution I finally decided upon evolved.

The Bank of Dave would ask its customers for permission to lend out their money. They would sign a certificate to this effect, which would also signify their agreement to two pages of complicated but necessary terms and conditions that I knew not a single customer would read. If they did, however, they would realise that they were signing up to a peer-to-peer lending scheme with a difference – a peer-to-peer lending scheme better than any other. For a start, I wouldn't be asking my customers to decide which businesses or individuals the bank should lend to. That was mine and David Henshaw's responsibility, and it would remain so. If the loans went bad, my customers' money would not be in danger. I would pay them their 5% no matter what, and I had a bulletproof insurance policy to reassure anyone who thought I might not. The risk was mine, not theirs.

From the point of view of my customers, there was hardly any difference between 'allowing' me to invest their money in return for 5% interest, and depositing their money in a bank. For them, the end result was the same. The Bank of Dave had finally found a way round all the ridiculous obstacles that had been put in its way. Admittedly, there was a bit more extra paperwork to do. Admittedly, we were having to tiptoe around all the obstacles the authorities were dropping on our path. But we had finally found a way of taking deposits from anybody, without the need for a banking licence. With one caveat: just as I was not allowed to call myself a bank, on no account was I allowed to use the word 'deposit'. If I did, it was porridge for breakfast.

Does that sound ridiculous to you? It does to me. From the very beginning of my journey with the Bank of Dave, I'd tried to do things properly. At every stage, I felt as though the authorities had tried to stop me. I was now in a situation where I could do everything a bank could do. I could lend money. I could accept money. I could pay more interest than any other bank in the country. I could personally guarantee all my customers' money – not just up to the limit of £85,000, but up to *any* limit. To all intents and purposes I was a real bank, taking real deposits from real people. The only difference was the bits of paper hanging on the wall of Burnley Savings and Loans allowing me to do all these things. As a result, I couldn't call myself a bank, and couldn't use the word deposits.

In order to do banking much better, I'd had to go it alone and find ways round the system. And I couldn't help wondering this: how bad does it have to be for us to reach the point where the *big* banks have to watch what they say and promise? How much more do they have to fuck up? How many more nest eggs do they have to lose, or bail-outs do they have to receive, before someone, somewhere admits that maybe – just *maybe* – there might be a different way of doing things and it's in nobody's best interests to try to stamp on anyone who has a go? Not a single one of the bankers who have lost so many millions has gone to prison for anything they've done, and yet I risked going straight to jail, without passing 'Go', for using one little word: 'deposit'.

The short-sightedness of the system almost beggared belief, but I was used to that. I could take comfort from the fact that all the red tape didn't make the blindest bit of difference to the ordinary people of Burnley. Finally, I could offer them the 5% interest on their savings that I'd always wanted to offer. All that remained was to let them know about it.

When a big bank wants to blow its own trumpet about a new offer for savers, it will spend tens of thousands advertising that product on TV and billboards all around the country. Well, I'm afraid the Bank of Dave didn't have the resources to hire Howard from the Halifax to do a song and dance routine. Even if we did, I wouldn't have spent it: every penny I wasted on a daft TV campaign was a penny I couldn't lend out. My budget for the launch was £250, to be spent on a £25 cash bonus for the first ten customers who took advantage of the

5%. As for publicity, we'd have to do it our own way...

We printed out some leaflets and I went down to Burnley market and started handing them out, talking to people and telling them about what I was doing. The following Saturday, I told them, I was opening up my 5% savings account offer. I was calling it Super Saver Saturday, and I'd love to see them. I'm pretty sure no bank manager has ever done anything like it, but I didn't care. I went on local radio – 2BR and BBC Radio Lancashire – to shout about Super Saver Saturday. I persuaded Burnley FC to supply some heavily discounted tickets to new customers. I used good, old-fashioned guerrilla marketing techniques, putting myself out there, banging my drum. I just hoped it would be enough to get people interested, and that they weren't too jaded with the whole industry to get as excited and motivated about the Bank of Dave as I was. On the Friday night before Super Saver Saturday, I was genuinely nervous. What if nobody turned up? What if we opened the doors of the bank on Saturday morning and there wasn't a soul waiting? What if all my hard work trying to figure out a way round all the ridiculous obstacles I'd encountered ended up being for nothing? I only had a couple of weeks left until my 180 days were over. What if the savings side of the Bank of Dave was, at the end of the day, a dead duck – just a way of making the rich richer? I felt as if my whole reputation was at stake.

The bank wasn't due to open on Super Saver Saturday until 10. I got there at 9.15. There was nobody waiting. Nobody queueing. My heart sank. I'd hoped that people would be beating a path to my door. I had been hoping that I'd caught the imagination of the inhabitants of Burnley. It looked like I was wrong.

Or maybe I wasn't, because there was in fact *one* person waiting. She was an elderly lady, and wasn't queueing on the pavement, but waiting in her little car outside the bank. I got talking with her, and found out that she was the daughter of the footballer Bob Lord. Bob was one of Burnley's most famous sons, a legend in the area. His daughter is now in her mid-seventies and she had wanted to queue up outside the bank, she couldn't because her legs were bad, so she'd been sitting and waiting in her little car. She'd been there since nine o'clock, and wondered if she could come in and sit in the warm. 'Of *course* you can,' I told her – I couldn't bear the idea that the Bank of Dave would keep her out in the cold until its doors officially opened. I let her in to the bank and sat her down with me behind the counter.

We sat there chatting, and as we did so, she put her hand on mine and told me that she *knew* her money would be safe with me, that she *wanted* me to take her savings and do good things with it. 'I want to be the first,' she said, and she handed over a cheque for a substantial sum of money. I can't tell you how heartwarming that felt. Even if nobody else turned up that day, at least I had one person wishing me all the luck in the world: an ordinary person, who wanted to be part of the change I was trying to bring about. A single person might not seem like a lot, but it was a start and meant the world to me. It gave me a huge boost of confidence, even though nobody else was there.

At quarter to ten there was still nobody outside. Ten to ten: nobody. Five to ten: nobody.

At three minutes to ten, they started to arrive. A queue of people appeared as if from nowhere – I guess they'd been waiting around in a nearby car park. And for the next three hours, the queue was constant. I had ordinary folk from all walks of life queueing out the door to hand over their money, entrusting it to the Bank of Dave. Some people put fifty quid in, one person put in £15,000. I knew it was a leap of faith for every single one of them, but it was a leap they seemed willing to take. At the end of our three-hour stint we'd taken nearly £62,000 of local people's money, and throughout the whole of Super Saver Saturday, not one person mentioned the words 'bank licence'. They were all told that I couldn't call myself a bank, but nobody cared. They didn't give two hoots that I couldn't call their deposits 'deposits'. Why? Because, like Bob Lord's daughter, they trusted me. I learned something that day. The success of my endeavour didn't just depend on me trusting the businesses and individuals to whom I lent money; it depended on my customers trusting me. I don't believe any of the big banks inspire that kind of trust in their clients. Perhaps they did once, but it has been eroded by their ineptitude and their greed. As we've already learned, trust is the financial system's most important commodity. The tenner in your wallet has no *real* value. It's only worth something because we say it is, and we trust everyone to agree on its value. So we can see that it's not just the banks that are knackered without trust. The very notion of money is too.

Super Saver Saturday was just the start. As I write this, we have a steady stream of punters coming through our doors, entrusting us with their money. Some of them have become regulars, giving us £25 or £50 a week, knowing that it's good for them and good for the local community. The sums aren't always huge in the grand scheme of things, but I know that for my customers they are significant. The Bank of Dave was always more about the pensioner with £35 to save than the rich bastard with 25 grand. It touches me every time I see someone place their money on the counter. It inspires me to graft even harder to ensure that every penny of their money works hard, not just for them, but for Burnley.

I'd done it. I'd found a way round the bullshit and socked it to the naysayers. I could lend money to struggling local businesses. Local people could deposit their money with me and earn many times more interest on it than they would in any other bank – or, as I ridiculously had to put it, I could 'help them achieve 5% on their savings' (not their deposits!). The Bank of Dave was the smallest in the country, but there was no doubt in my mind that it was also the best.

The 180th day arrived. And that morning, someone came to me with a problem that summed up everything the bank was about.

Paul Cherry is a loss adjuster. If you have an insurance claim – a fire in your house, or a flood, or the roof blows off in the wind – you can bet your boots that your insurance company will do everything in their power to pay out as little money as possible. They'll swear blind that your house is only worth this, your carpets are only worth that. When this happens, Paul is your knight in shining armour. He'll come along and deal with the insurance company for you, making sure you get the money and the service that is owing to you. Then – and this is the bit I really liked – he'll arrange local builders, plumbers and plasterers to come along and repair all the damage to your house that needs attention and, crucially, he'll wait for the cheque to come through from the insurance company so that you don't have to.

Paul had a problem. Sometimes the insurance companies are in the habit of holding back the money for as long as four months. The local builders, plumbers and plasterers will have forked out for the materials they needed to fix your house up, and now they're having to wait all this time for their money. It's an expense they can't afford to carry. Paul's dilemma was this: either he goes to the bigger construction companies based outside the area who can afford to wait for their money, and so takes the work out of the hands of local tradesmen. Or, he sets up a facility with a bank that would enable him to pay the local boys while he waits for the dear old insurance companies to cough up. The trouble was, he wasn't in a position to pay much money back on a weekly basis. He *had* to wait until he'd been paid by the insurance companies. He'd been to the big banks, but they weren't interested in helping him, not least because he had no security to back up the loan.

David H and I sat down with him to work out what we could do. There was no doubting that he had a great business. He'd been set up on his own for a few years and had been in the industry all his working life. He was clearly trustworthy and hardworking. But for me, the clincher was that he was trying to keep local people in work, and that he was helping a lot of older folk get their fair dues from the insurance companies.

We struck a deal. The Bank of Dave would make available to him a large sum of many thousands of pounds. He didn't have to take it all at once, but if he did take advantage of it, all he'd have to pay us was the monthly interest on the loan – he didn't have to worry about the capital. It worked out that a loan of £10,000 would cost him less than of £120 a month – not the cheapest money on the planet, but a fair deal, we thought, to help out someone we believed in who was just trying to do the right thing by people in his local community. When the money came through from the insurance companies, he'd pay us back. In the meantime, the Bank of Dave would be potentially lending out substantial sums without any security. Was I worried about that? Not really. I'd looked the man in the eye and I knew he was good for it. And from Day One, that was how the bank had done business the old-fashioned way.

Nobody was ever going to grow rich off the Bank of Dave. That was never the point. All I had ever hoped to do was prove that there was a better way to do banking. If I could demonstrate that there was, maybe other people with a few quid behind them could take the idea and run with it in their own communities. Maybe there could be the Banks of John, Phil and Sarah, all in different parts of the country, as well as the Bank of Dave. But why would anyone do this, if there wasn't a big, fat City bonus at the end of it? Setting up a bank is bloody hard work. Why bother if there isn't a pay day in it?

Nobody has a God-given right to wealth. I truly believe that. When people *do* earn fortunes, I think they have a responsibility to use them wisely. I count myself in this.

I've earned a few quid and I've done OK. But I know the time will come when I no longer get a kick out of running my businesses, and the thrill of sticking more zeroes on my bank balance no longer floats my boat. When that time comes, I have a plan. Nicky and I talk about it a lot. Across Africa, and the rest of the world there are hundreds of thousands of people who can't see for want of a simple cataract operation they cannot afford. So imagine this: a fleet of minibuses and trucks, kitted out with all the gear needed for the operation, and a team of doctors with the skills to perform it. Think how many lives could be improved by such a project. Patients could be helped into one of these mobile hospitals at one end, and walk out – unaided and able to see – from the other. Think of the difference my money could make. What could possibly be better than helping thousands of blind people to see again? It certainly seems a better use of money than ensuring that the next few generations of my children and grandchildren don't have to get up and go to work in the morning.

I'm no Bill Gates or Warren Buffett. I'm an ordinary bloke from Lancashire and my wealth, such as it is, is a drop in the ocean. But if everybody who has more money than they really need decided to put their minds to a bit of philanthropy, just imagine what could be done. And I think that the Bank of Dave goes to the very heart of this idea.

Greed isn't good. But money is. At least, it *can* be. I hope that the Bank of Dave has made that point, and that people who think that banking is rotten to its core can bring themselves to believe that it can be a uniquely positive force. I started this endeavour with a hunch. A hunch that it was possible to restore the average man in the street's faith in the banking system. A hunch that the decent, honest, ethical members of the community I lived in deserved better than they were getting. I think I succeeded in showing that those hunches were right. Our repayment rate – the number of people who do not default on their loans – is at the time of writing around 98%. Would it be better if we'd let a computer make our decisions for us instead of going out into the community, looking people in the eye and judging them in the old-fashioned way? Of course not. I think I have proved that the people of Lancashire are wonderful, trustworthy people. I think I've proved that if bankers do their jobs right by checking out people properly, going to see them and making decisions based on the people themselves and not on a load of figures on a computer screen, then there's no reason why the banks shouldn't be lending. If they took a leaf out of the Bank of Dave's book and started supporting small and medium-sized businesses, the economy will lift. There's nothing wrong with the people: the problem lies deep within the system.

Things need to change, but I'm not sure the Establishment really *wants* them to change. It's happy with its old boys' network, happy to be stuck with its own way of doing things. I can't help thinking that it is *scared* of change. Scared of me, and what I'm doing. So it should be, because I've got no plans to shut up about what I've learned. I've got a drum to bang, and I'm going to carry on banging it. At this very moment, at the David Fishwick Van and Minibus Sales garage in Colne, my guys are working on an old, white, part-exchange minibus. It's a vehicle with a difference. I call it my Battle Bus. I've fitted it out with a cash machine – so far as I know, it's the only cash machine on wheels in the world. The bus is only 18 inches shorter than the actual bank in Keir by Walk. It has a small safe and a similar desk and chairs where my customers can sit and talk to me about their needs. I want to get out on to the road, to spread the word about the Bank of Dave ethos. I see no reason not to park up outside the Bank of England, right in the heart of the City of London, and offer my services to people beyond the confines of Lancashire. I see no reason not to drive it to Strasbourg, where the European Parliament sits, and shout about what I've done to the politicians and decision-makers who might take on board that there is another way to do things, and that perhaps it isn't such a great idea to stand in the way of entrepreneurs and businessmen who might want to make a difference to other people's lives and help create change in the community.

I'm not fooling myself. I know mine is just a tiny bank. I know that the bigger banks have other issues to deal with that the Bank of Dave hasn't had to worry about – shareholders and big wage bills and higher overheads. Should bankers be allowed to make money? Of course they should. I've no argument with someone being paid a decent sum for a job well done. I just think that there needs to be a sense of proportion, and I don't believe there are many people outside the banking industry who agree that there is. And I honestly believe that the clever boys and girls in the City have something to learn from my 180 days in at the deep end. I honestly believe that it's not too late for them to stop their profit-at-any-cost strategies that have been so damaging to everyone, take a step back and remember why they're here and where they came from.

Just before we locked the door on the 180th day, an elderly couple from Nelson walked in. If you'd asked me to draw a picture of the kind of people I was looking at helping when I started this project, it would have been them, down to the old boy's flat cap and their Lancashire accents. They were the sweetest, nicest couple you could ever hope to meet. They explained that they'd wanted to come to Super Saver Saturday, but it had been their anniversary so they hadn't been able to. They had several thousand pounds' worth of savings, and they were getting next to nothing for it from their regular bank. They wanted to take advantage of our 5%.

Accepting money from this lovely old couple, knowing that their cash would help others and the interest they would earn would help them, seemed such a fitting end to my self-imposed timescale of 180 days – especially after agreeing a big, important loan that morning. It felt like we should celebrate. Down in the bank vault, there was a bottle of champagne left over from our opening six months previously. I didn't have any champagne glasses, and certainly wasn't going to waste the bank's money on buying some, so we cobbled together some wine glasses from the opening, blew the dust out of them and raised a glass to the Bank of Dave. I didn't doubt that if one of the big banks had something to celebrate, there would be an epic party costing hundreds of thousands at some swanky London venue. As far as I was concerned, they could keep that sort of knees-up. I was perfectly happy having a little gathering with David H, Chris, Mavis my bookkeeper and the old couple. A tiny bash for a tiny bank that was living within its means and doing things properly.

My 180 days were up and I was in profit. I'd completed the challenge I'd set myself. My little bank was up and running, and now that I'd proved it worked, I knew it would stay open for many years to come, looked after by proper, trustworthy people. Anyone with a pound to save in my local community could be sure they'd always have somewhere safe to put it. And anybody local who was struggling to borrow from the high street banks and needed a loan would have somewhere to go.

This isn't the end of the Bank of Dave. In fact, it's only the beginning. Now that I've shown that this model works it's time to pick a bigger fight. We need change in Britain. We need an alternative to the high street banks and we need it now. If the Bank of Dave has taught me one thing, it's taught me this: the only way to make change happen is to fight for it, to push yourself forward, to stand up, be counted and make yourself heard. So, if I have to go to London and park outside the Bank of England in my mobile bank and shout from the bloody rooftop, so be it. I am going to keep at the authorities to the point where they're sick of me and give in. Then they'll have to listen to me. We need to get the European courts to lift the blatant restriction of trade that stops small banks opening without putting down millions of pounds for the pleasure. So, if I need to take the fight to Europe, I will. If I need to park up in front of the European Parliament in Strasbourg, just you watch the Bank of Dave's Battle Bus give 'em hell! Like I said at the beginning of this book, banks are about people. I need people on my side. I need to go to Westminster and persuade as many lords, life peers and MPs as I possibly can to stand next to me. I already have some of them on my side, and I'm sure more will follow. But even more important than that, I need the help and support of the decent, honest, hardworking people of Britain. If I have that, then I'm unbeatable. By standing together we'll have defeated the bankers at their own game, and we'll get the change we so desperately need.

Remember: never give up; never, ever give up...

DF.

Acknowledgements

Huge thanks to: Nicola Fishwick; Conor and Sarah; Adam Parfitt; Ed Faulkner, Yvonne Jacob and all at Virgin Books; Barbara Levy; Ian Lilley; Katie Lander; Sue Summers; Steven Todd; Alison Pinkney; Loraine McKechnie; Becky Read; Claire Tippet; Daniel Brooks; Andrew Jackson, Jay Hunt, Sue Murphy, Saskia Wirth and all at Channel 4; Ted Robbins; Alison Brown; Sean Bannister; Franz and Mark; David Buick; Max Clifford, Louise Clifford, Victoria Cameron and all at Max Clifford PR; Keith Arrowsmith, Chris Moss and all at JMW Solicitor; Evan Davies; Alastair Campbell; Mark Barlow; Matthew Thompson; Andrew Stephenson, MP; Baroness Susan Kramer; Steven Baker, MP; Michael Meacher, MP; Guy Opperman, MP; John Jepps; Mark Mansour; Mark the Builder; Gary the Painter; Matt from Barrowford Safe and Lock Services; SMP Safes; Mark Lomas Office Supplies; Richard Slater; Tony Catterall; Mark Barlow; Mavis Mickleboro; Damian Chung; Samantha Smallridge; Keith Reynolds; Richard Peel; and Suleyman Terzi.